Native Children
and the Child
Welfare System

Native Children and the Child Welfare System

Patrick Johnston

Canadian Council on Social Development
in association with
James Lorimer & Company, Publishers
Toronto, 1983

ISBN 0-88862-639-8 paper
       0-88862-640-1 cloth

Design: Don Fernley

Canadian Cataloguing in Publication Data
Johnston, Patrick.
  Native children and the child welfare system
(Canadian Council on Social Development series)
1. Indians of North America — Canada — Child welfare.
2. Child welfare — Canada. I. Canadian Council on
Social Development. II. Title. III. Series.
E78.C2J64   362.7'9797071   C83-094146-0

The Canadian Council on Social Development
55 Parkdale Ave.
P.O. Box 3505, Station C
Ottawa, Ontario K1Y 4G1

Further copies of this book may be obtained from:

James Lorimer & Company Publishers
Egerton Ryerson Memorial Building
35 Britain Street
Toronto, Ontario M5A 1R7

Printed and bound in Canada

6 5 4 3 2   83 84 85 86 87 88

DEDICATION

This book is dedicated to the Pines — Vernon, Peter, Doug, Darryl, Dale and Mike — and to Lance Noley, who, although they may not know it, were the inspiration for this effort.

The research required to complete this book could not have been undertaken without the financial assistance provided by the following organizations. Their support is gratefully acknowledged.

The Canadian Council on Social Development
The Laidlaw Foundation
The Samuel and Saidye Bronfman Family Foundation
Petro-Canada
The United Church of Canada

CONTENTS

TABLES

FOREWORD

The Canadian Council on Social Development has taken great interest in child welfare since the council's very beginning in 1919, when it was called the Canadian National Council on Child Welfare. We have seen much progress during the last sixty years concerning the care of children unable to live with their own families. It has, however, become more and more evident that this progress has not benefitted Native children and their families. Several recent studies present a statistical description of the extent of the problem. Still, the questions are so complex that few people understand why or even how the system fails to fulfill its obligation to Native children. The CCSD is of the opinion that serious and immediate attention must be given to the shortcomings in the Canadian child welfare system and the way in which it affects Native Peoples. This book follows upon an earlier CCSD study, authored by Philip Hepworth, *Foster Care and Adoption in Canada*, in which the inadequacy of services to Native children was highlighted.

Program Director Patrick Johnston undertook an extensive consultation, ranging over two years, with Native groups, professionals, provincial and federal government officials, and experts in the field. His conclusions have been reviewed and endorsed by the CCSD board of governors, which has in turn undertaken that this issue should be followed on a continuing basis until improvements are evident.

T. Hunsley
Executive Director
Canadian Council on Social Development

ACKNOWLEDGEMENTS

Countless numbers of federal, provincial and territorial government officials, child welfare administrators, supervisors and caseworkers, academics and others have contributed to this work. In particular, I am indebted to Margie Cressman, Gweneth Gowanlock, Nancy Green, Kahn-Tineta Horn, Pete Hudson, Ruth Isaacs, Norm Levasseur, Brad McKenzie and Brad Morse.

Thanks are due also to members of an advisory committee who guided my efforts, especially Otto Driedger, Lorne Fidler, Calvin Pompano, Marion Sheldon and Judge Tillie Taylor.

The cooperation and assistance of Indian and Métis leaders, employees of many different Native organizations and, of course, the people they represent were essential and greatly appreciated. Special thanks to Cathie Bruyere, Clem Chartier, Helen Gladue, Mildred Gottfriedson, Keith Leclair, Eva MacKay, Elizabeth Paul, Bernice Robson, Russ Rothney, Conrad Saulis, Esther Seidl, John Sparrow and Greg Thompson.

I am also grateful to the staff of the Canadian Council on Social Development, in general, and to my secretary, Joanne Turcotte, in particular. She minimized many of the production difficulties and now knows almost as much about the subject of this book as I do. Thanks, as well, to Pam Kellaway and Steve Novosedlik, who assisted in the research.

Finally, there are several people who have demonstrated a tremendous personal commitment to improving the lives of Native families and children. The dedication and efforts of Chief Wayne Christian, Lyla MacEachern, Tim Maloney, Lance Sams and Chief Moses Tom were an inspiration. They have my thanks and my respect.

While all of the people cited above and others have helped me to complete this book, the observations and opinions it contains are mine alone, as are any of its errors.

A NOTE ON TERMS

The term "Native Peoples," which will be used throughout this book, is a generic one intended to include all of those people whose ancestors were indigenous to Canada. There are generally considered to be four subgroups, each of which will be described briefly here. The term "Native Peoples" will refer to all of them collectively.

It should be noted that, in some quarters, the term "Native" is considered to have a negative and demeaning connotation. The term "indigenous peoples" or "aboriginal peoples" is preferred. Such terms have not, however, become a part of our day-to-day language, and many groups still employ the word "Native" as part of their title — the Native Women's Association of Canada, for example. For these reasons the term "Native" will be used here.

Status Indians — those persons registered or entitled to be registered as an Indian under the terms of the Indian Act, a federal statute. The criteria for registration are not racial: they are legal and historical. Registration confers certain benefits and orders the relationship between the individual and the federal government in a unique way.

In some parts of Canada, the term "treaty Indian" is used synonymously with, or instead of, "status Indian." It refers to status Indians who belong to tribes which signed formal treaties with representatives of the Crown. There are some tribes who have never signed formal treaties, however, so while all treaty Indians are also status Indians, not all status Indians are treaty Indians. For this reason, the term "status Indian" will be used throughout this book to designate both treaty and non-treaty Indians registered under the Indian Act.

Non-Status Indians — those persons of Indian ancestry who, for a variety of reasons, lost or exchanged their right to be registered under the Indian Act.

Indians registered under the Indian Act can voluntarily give up their right to registration and the corresponding benefits and burdens by a process known as enfranchisement. Historically, enfranchisement brought with it certain benefits: for example, the right to vote, the right to consume liquor, et cetera. It was considered to be a reward to those Indians who had demonstrated that they were "worthy" of integration into the mainstream of Canadian life. Many non-status Indians are the offspring of registered Indians who enfranchised.

Métis — those persons of mixed Indian and European ancestry. They are the descendants of marriages between Indian women and early fur traders, who were primarily French and Scottish. The Métis are not included under the provisions of the Indian Act.

Inuit — those persons indigenous to the extreme northern sections of Canada. Inuit, an Inuktitut word meaning "the people," is now used in preference to the word "Eskimo." Constitutionally, Inuit are the responsibility of the federal government. They are not covered by the Indian Act, nor do they have a similar piece of legislation.

INTRODUCTION

On Thanksgiving Day, 1980, an estimated 1,000 people staged a protest in front of the Vancouver home of British Columbia's minister of human resources, Grace McCarthy. Most of the protesters were Indian, and many had travelled from different parts of the province in a march that became known as the Indian Child Caravan. The marchers were demonstrating their concern about the frequency with which provincial child welfare officials removed Native children from their own families and communities and placed them in non-Native foster and adoption homes.

Concern about the effects of the child welfare system on Native Peoples is not restricted to British Columbia. In fact, this issue is receiving increased attention across Canada because the highly disproportionate representation of Native children in the child welfare system is common to many provinces and territories. That phenomenon is the subject of this book.

One of the organizers of the Indian Child Caravan in B.C. was Wayne Christian, the chief of the Spallumcheen Band in the south-central region of the province. Christian is young, bright and politically astute. Because of his personal experience he also has a commitment to improving child welfare services for Native Peoples.

Christian related some of the details of his own involvement with the child welfare system in the eloquent and emotional speech he delivered in 1981 to a conference on Indian child welfare sponsored by the Canadian Indian Lawyers' Association.[1] Like many other Indian children in the 1960s and 1970s, he was taken from his parents and placed in a non-Indian foster home. He lived there until the age of 17 or so, at which time he returned to the reserve to live. Some of Christian's siblings were apprehended at the same time, including a younger brother who was sent to live with a different non-Indian family some distance from the reserve. Christian's brother eventually returned to live on the reserve as well. He had been unable to adapt to the non-Indian values and way of life in an urban setting, but his return to the reserve was not easy. He had been much younger when removed from his family and community, and his recollection of the Indian way of life was not as strong and powerful as that of his older brother.

Chief Christian spoke about his brother's struggle to determine his cultural identity. He described his own pain at recognizing that his brother, torn between two cultures and not being able to find a place in either, was going through hell. Even more painful was the fact that he was virtually powerless to help and was, ultimately, unsuccessful. One night Christian's mother told him of her premonition that something was seriously wrong. The next morning he found his brother dead from a self-inflicted gunshot wound.

Christian believes that his brother's death was the result of his treatment by the child welfare system. Actions ostensibly taken "in the best interests of the child" may have shortened his life. Through his involvement with others who joined the Indian Child Caravan,Chief Christian hopes to ensure that future generations of Native children will not have similar experiences.

The greater tragedy of Christian's story is that it is not that unusual. The apprehension of Indian children from his reserve was almost the norm when he was placed in a foster home. In fact, the Spallumcheen Band lost virtually an entire generation of its children to child welfare authorities. This experience was shared by many other Indian bands across the country and explains why some Native people consider the child welfare system to be an agent of cultural genocide.

The anger expressed by Native people about the damaging effects of Canada's child welfare services on Native children, families and communities was one factor that prompted this book. Another was the study *Foster Care and Adoption in Canada* by H. Philip Hepworth, which was published in 1980 by the Canadian Council on Social Development. Hepworth presented statistics which showed that the concerns of Native people were justified: a highly disproportionate number of Native children were caught up in the child welfare system. The final incentive for the book was provided at a workshop on child welfare held as part of the 1980 Canadian Conference on Social Development. Experts from across the country identified the issue of services for Native children and families as the single most important problem confronting Canada's child welfare system during the 1980s.

This book has been two years in the making, and yet it just skims the surface of an exceptionally complex issue. Some of the information it contains has been garnered from a traditional literature review, although there is a paucity of relevant documentation. Much of the factual information was obtained from federal, provincial and territorial officials by correspondence and personal interviews. All of this material,however, has been tempered with and complemented by field research. The author travelled extensively — especially through the four western provinces and nothern Ontario. Included were visits to a number of Indian reserves in several provinces. A special effort was made to talk with Native people about their own experiences with the child welfare system.

The first chapter will present a brief discussion of the history of child welfare services provided to Native Peoples and a detailed description of existing provincial and territorial policies. Chapter 2 will provide an updated statistical analysis of the extent to which Native children are represented in child welfare systems across the country. The subsequent chapter will discuss the various factors that contribute to the disproportionate number of Native children in care. Chapters 4 and 5 will present a variety of specific, constructive measures that can be taken to resolve the problem. The sixth chapter will describe several pilot projects in different parts of the country through which Native Peoples are becoming directly involved in providing child welfare services. The concluding chapter will suggest several emerging issues that may have the potential to alter the situation described in previous chapters.

In determining the content of the book, an effort has been made to provide something for everybody. Inevitably, some may find the material too technical and detailed, while others might be disappointed because it is not as comprehensive as they would like. It is hoped that at least some portion of the book will be of interest and use to everyone concerned about the issue, whether they be members of a reserve's child welfare committee or policy analysts and researchers.

In a landmark survey of contemporary Indians published in 1966, the principal author, H. B. Hawthorn, wrote:

> Public concern about the Indians and public knowledge of their problems that would demand a change are scanty and uneven. Public knowledge does not even match public misconception. Not enough is known of the problems to create a call for their solution.[2]

If nothing else, this book may help to educate the public about this one particular problem and to foster not only a call for, but action toward, solutions.

Notes to Introduction

[1] Leader Post (Regina), 20 March 1981. Another graphic and powerful description of the effects of apprehension on Native children is contained in a one-hour film documentary produced by Direction Films entitled *Our Children Are Our Future.*

[2] H. B. Hawthorn et al, *A Survey of the Contemporary Indians of Canada.* vol. 1 (Ottawa: Canada Department of Indian Affairs, 1966), p. 326.

CHAPTER 1

CHILD WELFARE AND NATIVE PEOPLES: PAST AND PRESENT

The inadequacy of the child welfare system as it now affects many Native people is of relatively recent vintage. It is a problem that has developed since the Second World War and didn't become apparent until the 1960s and 1970s.

This chapter will present a brief description of child welfare practices followed in the past with respect to Native people. It will also describe, in some detail, the current policies of each province and territory that govern the delivery of child welfare services to status Indian, non-status Indian, Métis and Inuit families and children. The link between past practices and present policies will be provided by a discussion of the jurisdictional dispute between the federal and provincial governments, which is key to an understanding of the problem.

PAST PRACTICES

Like most countries, Canada accepts the notion that the state has an obligation to care for children who, for whatever reason, cannot properly be cared for by their own parents. That reponsibility is enshrined in legislation that establishes a system of procedures and programs usually referred to as the child welfare system. It is this standard definition of child welfare that will be used here.

The activities governments undertake or mandate to care for neglected children are referred to as child welfare services. They include such things as adoption, placement in foster and group homes, the provision of family counselling and support services and aid to unmarried parents. Often such services are provided directly by government employees. In some cases, they are delivered by "independent" agencies, such as Children's Aid Societies (CAS),

1

which are mandated and funded almost exclusively by governments.

Canada is unique in that it does not so much have a system of child welfare as it has a number of child welfare systems—twelve systems, in fact. Since the British North America Act of 1867 first divided powers between the provincial and federal governments, child welfare has evolved as the exclusive responsibility of provincial and territorial governments.[1] As a result, each province and territory has its own child welfare legislation that defines its responsibilities and prescribes the services to be delivered. There are obviously similarities in services, but the ten provinces and two territories each have their own structure and method of delivering those services. The concerns of Native people can only be understood when it is realized that this country does not have a single, uniform system of child welfare.

The history of child welfare services for Native Peoples is a recent one. Forty years ago, Native people were much more isolated from the mainstream of Canadian society than they now are. They were less likely to move from reserves and remote communities into urban areas and were, consequently, less visible. Provincial child welfare departments and children's aid societies did not operate to any extent on reserves, and the number of Native children in the care of child welfare officials was minimal. As a result, the issue of child welfare and Native Peoples was of little concern or interest.

That is not to suggest, however, that some Native children were not in need of alternative care. On reserves, such children would sometimes be taken in and looked after by members of their extended family, which included aunts, uncles and grandparents. In some cases, the Indian agent, an employee of the federal government who supervised the activities on reserves, would place a child with another family on the reserve. Often they were simply sent to live in Indian residential schools.[2]

The end of the Second World War saw a tremendous proliferation of government operated and funded social services. This was a natural extension of a five-year period of war,when the preeminent role of government was acknowledged and accepted. At the same time, the profession of social work was gaining in credibility; its horizons were expanding, as many held the firm belief that in such endeavors lay the answers to world problems. Before long, attention was drawn to the child welfare services provided or, rather, not being provided to Native people.

In 1947, the Canadian Welfare Council and the Canadian Association of Social Workers submitted a joint presentation to a committee of the Senate and House of Commons appointed to

2

consider changes to the Indian Act. The brief addressed a variety of social service issues, including child welfare. It was critical of the situation of that time essentially because Native Peoples were not provided with services comparable in quality to those available to other Canadians.[3]

Referring to the role of the Indian agent in adoption, the brief said that "the practice of adopting Indian children is loosely conceived and executed and is usually devoid of the careful legal and social protection afforded to white children," and as wards of the federal government, "Indian children who are neglected lack the protection afforded under social legislation available to white children in the community."[4] The practice of placing neglected children in residential schools was also condemned.

The brief concluded that the best way to improve this situation was to extend the services of provincial departments of health, welfare and education to the residents of reserves. It recommended against the development of a federally operated service system parallel to those of the provinces and called on the federal government to confer with provincial authorities.

The extension of provincial child welfare and other social service programs seemed to be a logical way to overcome some of the problems facing the residents of reserves. The recommendation was obviously made with the best of intentions, but little attention was paid to the effect that extending provincial services would have on Indian families and communities. Nor did there appear to be any concern that provincial services might not be compatible with the needs of Indian communities.

Nevertheless, in 1951, major revisions to the Indian Act were introduced, including a clause that seemed to allow for the extension of provincial child welfare services. The changes, however, did not authorize additional funding to defray the cost of newly provided services, so over the ensuing years only some provincial child welfare programs were extended to residents of some reserves in some provinces.

The resulting confusion and disparity was acknowledged in H. B. Hawthorn's classic study of Indians published in 1966. In describing child welfare services available to Indians in most of Canada, Hawthorn said that "the situation varies from unsatisfactory to appalling."[5] He too concluded that the answer lay in the extension of provincial child welfare services, recommending that the provinces should be encouraged to extend all welfare services, including child welfare, and that Indians should be induced to accept them.[6]

THE JURISDICTIONAL QUESTION

In 1982 the child welfare situation for Native people, with some exceptions, could still be described as varying from "unsatisfactory to appalling." There has been a continual argument between the federal and provincial governments about which level of government has the legislative responsibility to provide child welfare services to reserves and which should pay.

The jurisdictional battle has most affected status Indians living on reserves. It has severely limited the access of families on some reserves to the full range of child welfare services provided by provinces, as Professor John MacDonald of the University of British Columbia noted in a 1981 review of child welfare for Native people in British Columbia.[7] The jurisdictional question is confusing and complex, but its importance cannot be underestimated, since it bears directly on the policies of provincial governments.

As previously discussed, there is no question that provincial governments have the legislative responsibility for child welfare while the federal government has responsibility for Indians. With respect to the provision of child welfare services to Indians on reserves, however, both levels of government absolve themselves and argue that the responsibility rests with the other party.

The federal government accepts its constitutional right and responsibility to legislate on behalf of Indians and to provide services. But it also argues that it can choose not to exercise that right, in which case the normal division of powers as spelled out in the British North America Act prevails. That option is given to the federal government, it believes, by Section 88 of the Indian Act, which was first included in the 1951 revision to the act. That clause reads as follows:

LEGAL RIGHTS

88. Subject to the terms of any treaty and any other Act of the Parliament of Canada, all laws of general application from time to time in force in any province are applicable to and in respect of Indians in the province, except to the extent that such laws are inconsistent with this Act or any order, rule, regulation or by-law made thereunder, and except to the extent that such laws make provision for any matter for which provision is made by or under this Act. R.S., c. 149, s. 87.[8]

Child welfare legislation, the federal government argues, are "laws of general application" and not inconsistent with the Indian Act. Therefore, the provincial government should be providing child welfare services on reserves.

Provincial governments, on the other hand, support their position by referring to Section 91.24 of the British North America Act, which reads:

VI. DISTRIBUTION OF LEGISLATIVE POWERS

Powers of the Parliament

91. It shall be lawful for the Queen, by and with the Advice and Consent of the Senate and House of Commons, to make Laws for the Peace, Order,and good Government of Canada, in relation to all Matters not coming within the Classes of Subjects by this Act assigned exclusively to the Legislatures of the Provinces; and for greater Certainty, but not so as to restrict the Generality of the foregoing Terms of this Section, it is hereby declared that (notwithstanding anything in this Act) the exclusive Legislative Authority of the Parliament of Canada extends to all Matters coming with the classes of Subjects next herein-after enumerated; that is to say....

24. Indians, and Lands reserved for the Indians....[9]

Some provinces interpret this section to mean that the federal government has the full responsibility to deliver services to Indians on reserves, and these provinces are reluctant to extend their child welfare services for that reason. Their position is often reinforced by organizations of status Indians that make the same argument. Many provinces will provide child welfare services to reserves, but only if compensated by the federal government. While the provinces are in agreement that the financing of services on reserves is a federal responsibility, Section 88 of the Indian Act does not clarify the financial obligations of the federal government to provinces that extend their services. As a result, the jurisdictional and financial arguments continue and the problem remains unresolved.[10]

The legality of these two diametrically opposite positions has never been contested in court. A decision rendered in 1979 by a provincial court judge in Manitoba, however, is often cited as evidence in support of the federal government. Judge J. Carson argued strongly that provincial governments not only have a responsibility to provide child welfare services on reserves, but, he suggested, they are guilty of unlawful conduct if they fail to do so. He stated:

It is now absolutely clear that it is the legal responsibility and duty of the province to supply child welfare services in accordance with the Child Welfare Act to the treaty Indian on the same basis and criteria as such services are supplied to the other residents of Manitoba.[11]

In spite of Garson's strong statement, it is not binding on the province. He was ruling only on an application by the director of child welfare for permanent guardianship of two status Indian children and offered his opinion on the jurisdictional question in the text of his judgment.

The issue of jurisdiction is not simply a dispute between the federal and provincial governments, however. The people most concerned, status Indians, have consistently taken the position that the federal government alone has the authority and responsibility for all services provided to Indian people.

The position of status Indians is also manifest in their deep mistrust of provincial government involvement in any issue that affects them. This suspicion has been especially prevalent since 1969, when the federal government attempted to overcome the inadequacy and contradictions in its previous policies towards Indians. It announced its new policy in the House of Commons by introducing a document entitled *Statement of the Government of Canada on Indian Policy, 1969.*[12]

The White Paper, as it came to be known, was a clear enunciation of the federal government's intention to change its relationship with Indian people. It implied that Indian people would achieve socio-economic equality with other residents of Canada only if they were treated on the same basis. To that end, the special status afforded Indian people was to be terminated, the Indian Act repealed, and the Indian Affairs bureaucracy dissolved.

In addition, the White Paper advocated that the responsibility for administering and delivering services to Indians be transferred to the provinces on the same basis as services were provided to other provincial residents. The White Paper advised retaining existing treaties, but they would be anachronistic and largely irrelevant. The federal government's responsibility would be limited to what it considered its legal obligations for unfulfilled treaty promises. In short, the federal government was proposing a wholesale policy of assimilation.

It is important to remember that, as angry and hostile towards the federal government as they may be at times, Indian people also believe that the protection afforded by federal legislation is their only means of survival. Until their economic position is stabilized and at least on a par with that of other Canadians, their very existence is threatened without the protection of the federal government.

The response of Indian people to the White Paper was swift and unequivocal. Certainly, they had concerns about some of the provisions of the Indian Act and the administration of Indian Affairs, but the abolition of their special status was not the solution. Elimination of the problem could be done without the elimination of Indians. As the National Indian Brotherhood stated, the White Paper would lead to "the destruction of a Nation of People by legislation and cultural genocide." In response to the government's argument that the White Paper was for discussion, Dave Courchene of the Manitoba Indian Brotherhood said, "We have not been consulted, we have been advised of decisions already taken. I feel like a man who has been told he must die and am now to be consulted on the method of implementing this decision."[13]

The message contained in the White Paper was clear. The federal government was quite prepared to end the protection afforded Indian people by federal legislation, even though it would result in the elimination of a unique and distinct, if fragile, culture. Although the White Paper was eventually shelved, it increased the mistrust and hostility Indians have long felt towards governments. To this day, many status Indians equate an extension of provincial services with assimilation.

The Indian people's suspicion of the provinces and the ongoing battle between the federal and provincial governments over jurisdiction have affected the nature and extent of child welfare services available to Native Peoples in different parts of the country. The fact that child welfare is the exclusive responsibility of the provinces and territories serves to further complicate the issue and explains the diversity of child welfare policies described below.

CURRENT CHILD WELFARE POLICIES [14]

Status Indians

British Columbia
Child welfare services are provided by the B.C. Ministry of Human Resources to residents of reserves in that province by way of an

informal, non-precedent-setting arrangement with the federal government that has existed since 1962. The agreement only covers child protection and child-in-care services, however, and does not include pre-protection services, such as daycare. The province charges the Department of Indian Affairs 100 percent of the costs incurred. The rate is escalated annually, using the escalator from the Established Programs Financing Act. In 1981-82 the rate was $23.80 per day per child.

The complete range of child welfare services is available to status Indian children and families living off-reserve, but Indian Affairs will only accept financial responsibility for the child-in-care costs if the parents of a status Indian child have not been self-sufficient off-reserve for one year.

There is one major exception to this agreement that dates from 1980. At that time the Spallumcheen Band near Enderby, B.C., assumed exclusive responsibility for child welfare for its members. The Spallumcheen case is an unusual and significant precedent and will be described in greater detail in chapter 6.

Alberta
The position of the Alberta government with respect to child welfare services on reserves appears to have evolved substantially in recent years. In 1980 a background paper prepared for Indian Affairs on the evaluation of child welfare services stated that, generally speaking, Alberta officials would provide services on reserves "only in the most extreme cases of neglect."[15] However the policy as of 1982 as described by Alberta officials, suggests that this is no longer the case.[16]

All reserves in Alberta are provided child protection services, that include response, investigation, assessment and counselling in cases of abuse or neglect, and foster or residential care placement for apprehended children. Adoption services are also included. In 1981 the province offered to pay operating costs for receiving homes on reserves if bands paid the capital costs.

Alberta extends these services, for the most part, without an agreement with the federal government. The province is reimbursed by Indian Affairs for status Indian foster children at a rate of $7.02 per day. Administrative costs are not included. The federal government also reimburses the province the per diem cost of services provided status children in group homes or institutions.

In some instances, an expanded range of child welfare services are available to residents of reserves in Alberta through trilateral

8

agreements. One of these, which involves the Blackfoot Band of the Gleichen Reserve, will be described in chapter 6.

Bands are also eligible, as are municipalities, to apply for funding to the Family and Community Support Services (FCSS) Program, which provides up to 80 percent of operational funding for programs oriented toward primary preventive care. Funding is allocated on a per capita basis, and the additional 20 percent must be provided by the band. The range of services that may be funded include nursery schools, mothers'-day-out and family life education programs, among others. The services are provided by an agreement between the province, the band and/or Indian Affairs. Although only two bands had taken advantage of the FCSS program as of May 1982, several others were considering it.

The situation in Alberta, in other words, has altered since the mid to late 1970s. While all of the services offered by Alberta's child welfare branch are not provided to residents of reserves, it is obvious that assistance is available in many instances other than "extreme cases of neglect."

The full range of services are available, however, to status Indians living off-reserve. There is no formal agreement with the federal government, but the financial arrangements are the same as those described above. All other costs are borne by the provincial government.

Saskatchewan

The effects of the jurisdictional dispute are, perhaps, more apparent in Saskatchewan than anywhere else. That province has consistently taken the position that the provision of child welfare services on reserves is a federal and not a provincial responsibility. Saskatchewan's stance is supported by the Federation of Saskatchewan Indians (FSI), which is an important force in provincial politics. As a result, no agreements exist, formal or informal, between the bands, the province or the federal government. The province may provide limited child welfare services, but only in instances where Indian Affairs is unable or unwilling to provide the needed services. This is true of the Department of Northern Saskatchewan (DNS) which provides child welfare services to all residents of northern Saskatchewan, and of Saskatchewan Social Services, which has that responsibility in the rest of the province.

Generally speaking, the band councils and/or Indian Affairs employees attempt to provide child welfare services, but they have neither the resources nor the training to do an adequate job. Nor do they have the statutory powers of apprehension vested with provincial child welfare officials. They can remove a child only with parental consent. If the situation reaches a critical point and apprehension is necessary to protect the child, then provincial officials may intervene. This situation is often characterized as a "life and death" approach to child welfare.

The reluctance of the province, as of 1982, to become involved on reserves, except in life and death situations, is not a new position. In fact, it has been policy since the 1960s. A 1980 policy statement read:

> As early as 1962 a directive was issued to field staff to accept protection referrals only in extreme cases of neglect. The department's policy on providing protection services on Indian reserves has essentially remained unchanged since the 1962 policy directive.[17]

Many people concerned about the welfare of children were, and still are, very concerned about Saskatchewan's policy. One such person, Dr. Mildred Battel, worked for the Saskatchewan government from the mid-1940s to the mid-1960s and was director of child welfare at one point. She described the situation as follows:

> We took very few Indian children into care. Our policy was very harsh. We interfered if the social worker (Indian Affairs) thought a child was in physical danger. It was horrible because how did you know when a child was dying? But that was policy when I left the department in 1965, and I don't think it has changed much.[18]

With respect to child welfare services for status Indian children living off-reserve, the official policy is similar. Saskatchewan Social Services will provide child welfare services whenever the federal government is unwilling or unable to provide such services. The province considers the federal government to be 100 percent financially responsible and bills Indian Affairs for the full cost of provincial services provided to status Indian children.

The Department of Nothern Saskatchewan policy differs to some extent. DNS officials have stated that they are even less likely to extend services to status residents off-reserves.[19] For all intents and purposes, the whole DNS catchment area is considered a "reserve." They will become involved in child welfare matters affecting status children whether on- or off-reserve only if Indian Affairs officials are unable or unwilling and if the need is "urgent." One DNS official pointed out that this strained the working relationship between provincial and federal officials and described it as "an unworkable situation."[20]

Manitoba

The policy (as of 1982) of Manitoba's Department of Community Services and Corrections regarding child welfare and Native Peoples is in a state of flux. Historically, there were essentially two different policy positions. For residents of most reserves in central and northern Manitoba, the situation has been somewhat similar to that of Saskatchewan. Only limited child welfare services (primarily protection) were provided by provincial officials to these bands, which accounted for approximately 75 percent of all bands in Manitoba.

The situation was very different, however, for the remaining 14 bands located in southern Manitoba. They had access to the full range of services provided by the Children's Aid Societies of western, eastern and central Manitoba. This arrangement was the result of a bilateral agreement signed by the federal government and Manitoba in 1966. Manitoba was totally reimbursed by Indian Affairs for the per diem cost of maintenance and supervision of children. An additional amount was allocated for assistance to unmarried mothers and family services.

All of this has changed substantially as a result of a tripartite agreement signed in February 1982 by the federal government, Manitoba and the Four Nations Confederacy. The agreement replaces the 1966 arrangement and allows for the transference of the administrative reponsibility for providing child welfare services on reserves to Indian authorities operating under the authority of Manitoba legislation. This agreement was pre-dated by the establishment of the Dakota-Ojibway Child and Family Services (DOCFS) in 1981, Canada's first recognized Indian-controlled child welfare agency. In July of that year, the authority for providing services to certain bands in southern Manitoba was formally transferred from the three CASs to the DOCFS. A description of the specifics of both the Canada-Manitoba-Indian Child Welfare Agreement and the DOCFS will be found in chapter 6.

Manitoba does provide child welfare services to status Indians living off-reserve on the same basis as they are provided to non-Indian residents. They are cost-shared with the federal government under the Canada Assistance Plan (CAP), as are welfare services provided to all Manitobans.

11

Ontario

All child welfare programs in Ontario are administered and delivered by a province-wide network of Children's Aid Societies. Their services are also extended to all reserves in Ontario as a result of a 1965 formal bilateral agreement between the provincial and federal governments. The *Memorandum Respecting Welfare Programmes for Indians* covered a variety of programs only one of which was child welfare. All child welfare services offered by CASs are included, and the province recovers from the federal government 95 to 97 percent of the total cost involved.

The 1965 memorandum applies only to status Indians with reserve status. Status Indians living off-reserve, however, have access to the same child welfare services available to other Ontario residents with the federal government's reimbursement by way of the Canada Assistance Plan.

In 1977 a tripartite review of social services delivered to Indian residents as a result of the 1965 memorandum was begun by representatives of the federal and provincial governments and Indian organizations in Ontario. The review has resulted in two major reports: *A Starving Man Doesn't Argue* and *Community Care—Indian Control of Indian Social Services.*

The latter report presents a six-stage typology that would result in an Indian-controlled system of child welfare for Indian children. The Ontario government has supported an increased role for Indians in the planning, administration and delivery of services. It has stated, however, that any changes must be made within the context of the 1965 memorandum and its division of responsibilities between the federal and provincial governments. The Ontario government has no plans to renegotiate the 1965 agreement.

Concurrently with, or perhaps as a result of, the Social Service Review, Ontario's Ministry of Community and Social Services (COMSOC) has developed a Native Child Welfare Prevention program. Designed to respond to the need for community-based child welfare services expressed by both Indian bands and Indian political associations, the prevention program is a joint venture of the province, Children's Aid Societies and Indian bands. Indian involvement is required, and the program design, staffing, budget and evaluation is jointly undertaken by all three parties. In 1981 agreements to fund this program were made with eight CASs and 21 Indian bands. The development of the Native Child Welfare Prevention Program by the District of Kenora CAS has been detailed in chapter 6.

Quebec

Since the 1970s, a majority of Indians living on reserves in Quebec have been provided with child welfare services delivered by regional social service centres. Agreements have been signed between individual band councils, social service centres, and Indian Affairs. They cover a broad range of services and include the full range of child welfare programs. There is extensive and direct involvement of Indian people, both in the planning and delivery of services to reserves. The cost of services to reserve residents is totally subsidized by the federal government.

It is anticipated that negotiations under way in 1982 may alter this situation to some extent and that the Attikimak-Montagnais Council (AMC) will sign agreements with social service centres on behalf of individual bands representing the Attikimak and Montagnais people when they come up for renewal in 1982-1983. It is hoped that the greater resources available to the AMC will allow it to assist in the improvement of services to all Attikimak and Montagnais and will foster the development of a policy of "Indianization" of the services.

The major exception to the arrangement described here involves the approximately 6,500 Crees of northern Quebec. In 1975 the Cree and Inuit signed what is now known as the James Bay Agreement with Quebec and the federal government. In return for a cash settlement, the Cree and Inuit gave up their rights to a large land mass.

One of the provisions of the James Bay Agreement allowed for the gradual transfer of responsibility for health and social services provided to the Cree from the federal to the provincial government. The transfer, which included responsibility for child welfare, was to have been completed by 31 March 1981. Since that date, Quebec's Ministry of Social Affairs has been responsible for providing all of the services mandated by the provincial Health and Social Services Act. Costs for all such services, including child welfare, are shared between Quebec and the federal government.

The actual delivery of social services to the Cree is done through a decentralized body known as a regional health and social services council. The council is governed by a board of directors consisting primarily of Indian people. In most cases, Indian community social workers provide child welfare services to small, isolated Cree communities in northern Quebec.

The James Bay Agreement has received a great deal of criticism, primarily from the Cree who signed it. They have charged that both levels of government have not respected the agreement and have not

13

provided the kinds and quality of services stipulated. After two children died of gastroenteritis in 1980, the Cree launched suits against both governments. After an investigation by federal officials, the Minister of Indian Affairs, John Munro, provided an additional $61.4 million. The concerns of the Cree have primarily been restricted to housing and sanitation and have not appeared to include child welfare.

Status Indians in Quebec who do not live on reserves have access to the child welfare services provided by community social service centres to all Quebec residents. All such services are cost shared by Quebec and the federal government.

New Brunswick

Although a formal agreement does not exist between New Brunswick and the federal government, provincial child welfare services are extended to residents of reserves as required or requested. All services provided to other residents are available, including protection, child care, unmarried parents and adoption services. Indian Affairs reimburses the province for the per diem and supervision costs of status children in care. The cost of other services are recovered through the Canada Assistance Plan. This arrangement applies as well to status Indians living off-reserve in New Brunswick.

The New Brunswick Department of Social Services has entered into agreements with four reserves to deliver a variety of personal social services, such as homemaker services, which are seen as being complementary to child welfare. The cost is absorbed by the province with partial recovery through CAP. Tripartite discussions have been taking place for several years to formally establish a child welfare agreement, and one similar to the Canada-Manitoba-Indian Child Welfare Agreement may be signed in the near future.

Nova Scotia

In 1964 a memorandum of agreement was signd by Canada and Nova Scotia that stipulated that Indians living on reserves in Nova Scotia would receive the same child welfare services provided to other residents. Included are assessment, counselling, child protection and placement services, homemaker and daycare services, research and evaluation. The federal government reimburses the province for 100 percent of all costs incurred for the care and custody of status Indian children and 100 percent of related administrative costs. This same arrangement extends to status Indians living off-reserve.

Prince Edward Island
Prince Edward Island does not have an agreement with the federal government but does extend child protection services to reserves. In most cases, provincial officials go on to reserves in response to a request from the chief or a welfare officer.

Indian Affairs reimburses the province for the per diem costs related to foster care. The administrative costs are not covered.

Newfoundland and Labrador
There has existed since 1965 an agreement between the federal government and Newfoundland and Labrador to extend provincial child welfare services to Native people in that province. The position of Native people in Newfoundland and Labrador is unique, however, and necessitates a brief history lesson.

Prior to Newfoundland's entry into Confederation in 1949, people of Indian ancestry were considered to be full citizens like any other. Newfoundland did not want to change that situation, and, as a result, the terms of union are silent on the responsibility for the Indian peoples.

In the early 1950s', however, the federal government recognized that it had a special responsibility to the people of Indian ancestry in Newfoundland and Labrador, who were extremely disadvantaged. Thus, the federal government signed several agreements by which the province would extend its services to several designated Indian communities. (There are no reserves.) In most cases such services were not previously available because of the isolation of Indian communities. This arrangement allowed the province to extend its child welfare services to Indian communities and is the basis of the 1965 agreement. The provincial share of the cost is 10 percent, with the federal government providing the remainder.

The Northwest Territories
All status Indians in the Northwest Territories receive the complete range of child welfare services provided by the NWT Department of Social Services. The financial arrangements are included in the overall federal/territorial financial agreement and there are no special provisions relating only to child welfare.

The Yukon Territory
In 1961 the federal government and the Yukon Territory signed an agreement which stipulated that the full range of child welfare services provided by the Yukon government be offered to all status Indians. The

services included protection, family counselling, foster and group home care, adoption services, and so on. The agreement applied equally to all status Indians whether living off or on a reserve.

The federal government reimburses the Yukon for 100 percent of the actual cost of services to status Indian children in care. The agreement also includes provision for a fixed dollar payment to the Yukon to cover administrative costs.

The Yukon territorial government, the federal government, and the Council of Yukon Indians were engaged as of late 1982 in discussions about land claims settlements. Although the issue of social programs has entered the discussion, it is not expected that an eventual settlement would substantially alter the territorial policy as described here.

Non-Status Indians and Métis

A dispute over jurisdiction does not affect the delivery of child welfare services for non- status Indian and Métis children and families in the same way that it does for status Indians. Jurisdiction is still an issue, however — especially for non-status Indian and Métis leaders.

All provinces and territories offer the full range of their child welfare services to non-status Indians and Métis on the same basis as they are offered to all other residents. In some instances, child welfare departments may have informal policies which pertain primarily to Native people. Many jurisdictions state, for example, that attempts are made to place a Native child in a Native setting in recognition of the importance of the child's culture. There are few, if any, formalized policies directed exclusively at non-status Indians or Métis children, however, and there appears to be a great reluctance to establish such provisions.

Most provinces and territories consider non-status Indians and Métis simply to be members of one of many different minority groups, and they consider their child welfare legislation, policies and practices to be broad and flexible enough to accommodate the needs of all children. Special provisions for minority groups are not necessary, the argument goes, and may even be harmful. The creation of separate categories of children has the potential for unequal and discriminatory treatment. It would be unjust to single out non-status Indians and Métis for special treatment, most provinces would argue, because their status is no different than that of other minority groups.

Many non-status Indians and Métis would disagree strongly with the proposition that they are no different than other minority groups. They have argued in the past that they are the responsibility of the federal government and should be considered and treated as Indians under the terms of the constitution.[21]

This issue has become even more clouded since the patriation and passing of the Constitution Act, 1981 which contained special provisions for aboriginal peoples who were defined to be Indian, Inuit and Métis peoples. There was even an attempt in the autumn of 1982 to establish a seperate alliance of Métis organizations distinct from bodies which also included non-status Indians. Those who support such a move believe that, according to the provisions of the new constitution, there is no such thing as a non-status Indian. There are only Indians, Métis and Inuit, all of whom, as of 1981, have a unique and distinct relationship with the rest of Canadian society.

The precise nature of this relationship has yet to be defined. The Constitution Act 1981 may have altered the legal position of non-status Indians and Métis, however, and that, in turn, may affect the future delivery of child welfare services.

Inuit

There are no more than 25,000 Inuit in all of Canada, and the vast majority of them live in the Northwest Territories, northern Quebec and Labrador. For the very few Inuit in other jurisdictions who come into contact with the child welfare system, the services provided are exactly the same as those available to others in that province or territory.

The responsibility for providing child welfare services to Inuit in the Northwest Territories, where most live, rests with employees of the territorial Department of Social Services. The federal government provides financial assistance by way of the overall federal/territorial financial agreement rather than by a separate agreement.

Inuit children of Labrador are the responsibility of Newfoundland and Labrador's Child Welfare Branch. The federal government has entered into special financial arrangements to assist the province in extending its child welfare services to remote Inuit communities. The funding is provided using a per capita formula, with the figure of two-thirds of the population in Inuit commuities being used as a base to exclude non-Inuit residents. The federal contribution then amounts to approximately 90 percent of program costs.

As a result of the James Bay Agreement of 1975, Quebec's Ministry of Social Affairs has exclusive jurisdiction to provide all health and social services to the Inuit in the Hudson's Bay and Ungava Bay area of northern Quebec. As with the Cree, all services, including child welfare, are provided by means of a decentralized body with extensive involvement of Inuit people in the design and delivery of services.

As it may affect non-status Indians and Métis, the Constitution Act, 1981, may also potentially alter the relationship between the Inuit and the rest of Canada's population. Although it remains to be seen whether this will affect child welfare services, there should be some indication in this regard in the spring of 1983. At that time, a meeting of Canada's first ministers will be convened to define the aboriginal rights of the Indian, Métis and Inuit peoples that are now enshrined in the new constitution.

Placement of Native Children Outside Canada

If there is one issue in particular relating to Native child welfare about which there is a great deal of confusion and misunderstanding, it is the extent to which Native children are placed in foster and adoption homes in the United States. One of the questions asked of provincial and territorial deputy ministers of social services during the research for this book related specifically to their departmental policy with respect to this practice (see appendix A). The responses were virtually identical. There was either a policy in place or an "unwritten rule" prohibiting such placements. In almost all cases, responses indicated that no, or very, very few Native children have been placed in the U.S. since the late 1970s.

The exception was Manitoba, which reported that, in 1980, 54 Native children were placed in the U.S. That compared with 71 Native children in 1975. Since that time, and in response to the anger expressed by Native leaders, Manitoba has instituted a moratorium on the placement of Native children outside the country.

As of mid-1982, therefore, policies or practices in effect in all jurisdictions in Canada prohibited the placement of Native children in foster or adoption homes in the United States except in unusual circumstances. Nevertheless, there continue to be allegations made that Native children from Canada are being "marketed" in the U.S. in large numbers.

Many such assertions come from Americans. They claim that the demand for Indian babies has increased since the 1978 U.S. Indian Child Welfare Act prohibited the adoption of Indian children by non-Indians. Non-Indian families in the U.S. who want to adopt Indian children must now look to Canada. The accuracy of these claims is difficult to determine. Some are backed by evidence dating from the late 1960s and early 1970s. At that time, Manitoba was not alone in placing Native children across the border; it was a practice followed in other jurisdictions. Since that time, however, prohibitions have been introduced. It is misleading to judge the 1982 situation, in other words, using statistics that are more than five years old.

It may also be the case that those in the U.S. making such claims are only familiar with the Manitoba situation. They may have incorrectly assumed that Manitoba's practice (until 1982) of placing Native children in the U.S. was one also pursued by the other provinces and territories.

This is not to deny that there are many Native children in foster and adoption homes in the U.S. who are originally from Canada. An official from the state of Maine, for example, estimates that almost one-half of Indian children in their care have some affiliation with Canadian bands.[23] There are at least two explanations.

In the first place, many of these children may initially have been placed in the U.S. as infants ten or more years ago when the practice was more common in Canada. Secondly, some of those children may have been apprehended by American child welfare officials after their parents had moved to the U.S. from Canada. This is particularly true of border states, where tribes straddle the international boundary and where there is a fair degree of movement back and forth.

It is important to bear in mind that child welfare programs in the U.S. have been severely affected by the cutbacks instituted by the Reagan administration since 1980. State officials have to pare their child welfare costs substantially, and one of the ways is to reduce the number of children in care. One method of doing this is to return Canadian Indian children to their province of origin. This is clearly being attempted by some states. In the process, they may be fanning the flames of protest that are based on incorrect or out-of-date information.

All of the evidence suggests that the placement of Native children from Canada with foster or adoptive families in the U.S. is a practice no longer followed in Canada to any significant extent. If it is still happening, it is being done unofficially and/or illegally.

Summary

This somewhat detailed description of current provincial and territorial policies may serve to show if nothing else, how complex is the subject of child welfare services for Native Peoples. The issue of services for status Indian children and their families is particularly complicated and is compounded by the jurisdictional dispute between the federal and provincial governments. The end result is an incredible disparity in the quantity and quality of child welfare programs available to status Indians from one province to another. In some instances, there is a disparity within a single province. This myriad of differing policy approaches results in unequal treatment of Indian children across Canada.

It is important to remember, of course, that there are often differences between official policy and actual practice. What is supposed to happen in theory does not always coincide with what takes place in reality. This distinction was noted by a former employee of Manitoba's Department of Community Services and Corrections, among others.[24] He worked in east-central Manitoba where the relations between department officials and the bands were very good. Child welfare services were made available to those bands even though Manitoba's official policy was one of very limited service. This particular employee stated that this kind of relationship did not exist in most other regions in central and northern Manitoba, where a "life and death" approach was more common.

On the other hand, status Indians in particular may not have the benefits of a full range of child welfare services even in provinces that make them available to reserves. Indian people may not trust child welfare officials and political pressure may be exerted on band councils, preventing them from taking advantage of programs for which they are eligible—especially those operated by the provinces.

It is clear from this review that existing provincial and territorial policies concerning the provision of child welfare services to Native Peoples are incredibly varied. This, in itself, is not necessarily a bad thing. Obviously, what is more important is the effect of such policies on the people for whom they are designed. Some of those effects will be described in the next chapter.

Notes to Chapter 1

[1] For a concise listing of the key developments in child welfare province by province, see H. Philip Hepworth, *Foster Care and Adoption in Canada* (Ottawa: Canadian Council on Social Development, 1980), pp. 10-17.

[2] H.B. Hawthorn et al, *A Survey of the Contemporary Indians of*

Canada, vol. 1 (Ottawa: Canada Department of Indian Affairs 1966), p. 326.

[3]Canadian Welfare Council and Canadian Association of Social Workers, "Joint Submission to the Special Joint Committee of the Senate and the House of Commons Appointed to Examine and Consider the Indian Act" (Ottawa: Canadian Welfare Council, 1947), p. 3.

[4]Ibid., p. 6.

[5]Hawthorn, *Survey,* p. 327.

[6]Ibid., p. 339

[7]John A. MacDonald, *"The Spallumcheen Indian Band By-Law and Its Potential Impact on Native Indian Child Welfare Policy in British Columbia"* (Vancouver: School of Social Work, University of British Columbia, April 1981), p. 5.

[8]*Revised Statutes of Canada 1970,* C. I-6, s. 88.

[9]Ibid., 1970, Appendices, No. 5, s. 91 (24).

[10]For a concise description of the jurisdictional dispute, see J.Rick Ponting and Roger Gibbins, *Out of Irrelevance: A Socio-Political Introduction to Indian Affairs in Canada* (Toronto: Butterworths, 1980), pp. 182-84.

[11]Director of Child Welfare v. B, 6 W.W.R. 229 (1979).

[12]Government of Canada, *Statement of the Government of Canada on Indian Policy, 1969* (Ottawa: Canada Department of Indian Affairs and Northern Development, 1969).

[13]Sally M. Weaver, *Making Canadian Indian Policy: The Hidden Agenda 1968-70* (Toronto: University of Toronto Press, 1981), pp. 174-75.

[14]The information in this section was gleaned from the following sources: Canada, Department of Indian and Northern Affairs, "Background Paper for the Evaluation of Child Welfare Services" (Ottawa, 1980); idem, "Briefing Note: Child Welfare Services for Indian Families and Children" (Ottawa, 1980); and responses to a questionnaire about policies affecting the provision of child welfare services to Native Peoples that was sent to all provincial and territorial departments of social services (See Appendix A.)

[15]Canada, Department of Indian and Northern Affairs, "Background Paper for the Evaluation of Child Welfare Services" (Ottawa, 1980), p. 17.

[16]Correspondence from Amelita A. Armit, Acting Assistant Deputy Minister, Planning Secretariat, Alberta Department of Social Services and Community Health, 13 May 1982.

[17] Saskatchewan, Department of Social Services, "Policy Statement: Department of Social Services" (Regina, 9 July 1980), p. 8.

[18] In correspondence to the author, 11 March 1982. The writer has also provided a useful history of child welfare in Saskatchewan in her book *Children Shall Be First: Child Welfare Saskatchewan, 1944-1964* (Regina: Published with the assistance of the Saskatchewan Department of Culture and Youth, 1979).

[19] Correspondence from Roy Rysavy, Assistant Director, Social Services Branch, Department of Northern Saskatchewan, 28 April 1982.

[20] In conversation with the author, April 1982. Since that conversation, Saskatchewan elected a Conservative government. The new government announced its intention to phase out the Department of Northern Saskatchewan, in which case the responsibility for child welfare would probably be transferred to Saskatchewan Social Services, which would then have a province-wide jurisdiction.

[21] Harry W. Daniels, *We Are the New Nation: The Métis and National Native Policy* (Ottawa: Native Council of Canada, 1979), pp. 6 - 7.

[22] Correspondence from R.D. Johnstone, Manitoba Deputy Minister of Community Services and Corrections, 21 January 1982.

[23] Correspondence from Nancy Goddard, Division of Child and Family Services, Department of Human Services, Maine, U.S.A., 9 October 1981.

[24] In conversation with the author, September 1981.

CHAPTER 2
THE SIXTIES SCOOP

Most of the existing federal-provincial agreements with respect to child welfare services for Native people date from the early and mid-1960s. It is not simply coincidence that a phenomenal increase in the number of Native children being apprehended from their families and taken into the care of child welfare authorities occurred at the same time.

There is a scarcity of reliable data on Native children in care during the 1950s and 1960s, but statistics compiled by British Columbia officials give us an indication of a profound change in the composition of the child-in-care population.

In 1955 there were 3,433 children in the care of B.C.'s child welfare branch. Of that number it was estimated that 29 children, or less than 1 percent of the total, were of Indian ancestry. By 1964, however, 1,446 children in care in B.C. were of Indian extraction. That number represented 34. 2 percent of all children in care.[1] Within ten years, in other words, the representation of Native children in B.C.'s child welfare system had jumped from almost nil to a third. It was a pattern being repeated in other parts of Canada as well.

One longtime employee of the Ministry of Human Resources in B.C. referred to this process as the "Sixties Scoop."[2] She admitted that provincial social workers would, quite literally, scoop childen from reserves on the slightest pretext. She also made it clear, however, that she and her colleagues sincerely believed that what they were doing was in the best interests of the children. They felt that the apprehension of Indian children from reserves would save them from the effects of crushing poverty, unsanitary health conditions, poor housing and malnutrition, which were facts of life on many reserves. Unfortunately, the long-term effect of apprehension on the individual child was not considered. More likely, it could not have been imagined. Nor were the effects of apprehension on Indian families and communities taken in account and some reserves lost almost a generation of their children as a result.

There are some observers, however, who do not believe that the Sixties Scoop of Indian children by child welfare authorities was simply an accident or the consequence of social workers' increased sense of compassion.[3] Rather, they consider it simply a new wrinkle in the process of colonialization that has characterized the treatment of Native people since Europeans first arrived on this continent. One element in that process is the devaluation of and inferior status accorded to the customs and practices of the group colonialized by the dominant culture.

Proponents of this theory point out that in the first half of this century government agencies institutionalized colonialization by removing Indian children from their parents at an early age and placing them in residential schools. In time, it became obvious that education was not the only objective of residential schools. Stories of Indian children being beaten for speaking their own language seeped into the public consciousness and, eventually, began to discredit the residential school system. Gradually, as education ceased to function as the institutional agent of colonialization, the child welfare system took its place. It could continue to remove Native children from their parents, devalue Native custom and traditions in the process, but still act "in the best interest of the child." Those who hold to this view argue that the Sixties Scoop was not coincidental; it was a consequence of fewer Indian children being sent to residential schools and of the child welfare system emerging as the new method of colonialization.

However one chooses to explain the Sixties Scoop, there is no question that the number of Native children coming into care increased dramatically in the 1960s both in absolute and relative terms. What is also clear is that this phenomenon changed very little in the 1970s, as the balance of this chapter will show. By 1980 it was still the case in many jurisdictions that a highly disproportionate number of Native children were in the care of child welfare authorities. In some cases the numbers of Native children in care are astoundingly high and represent more than a majority of all children in care. In virtually all instances, the percentage of Native children in care is much higher than their proportion of the total child population. A breakdown of some of these statistics by province and territory is provided below.

THE STATISTICAL PICTURE

The tables presented in this chapter have been compiled from information provided by the Social Development Directorate of Indian and Northern Affairs in Ottawa and in the responses to a survey sent to all provincial and territorial deputy ministers of social services (see Appendix A). In order for the data to be fully understood by the reader, however, a number of qualifications must be made.

In the first place an inter-provincial/territorial comparison of child welfare statistics is instructive but only to a point. Such comparisons are limited for a number of reasons. For example, the age of children covered by child welfare statutes varies considerably. In some provinces, child welfare statistics only include children under the age of 16. In others, they extend to children under the age of 19.

In addition, the nature of the services provided and considered to be part of a child welfare program differs from province to province. In some cases, children may receive a service in their own homes and will be counted in the children "in care" statistics even though they are not physically in care. In other provinces, those children would not be included in the children-in-care figures.

To further complicate matters, there is an incredible disparity from jurisdiction to jurisdiction in the collecting and reporting of child welfare data. For example, there are a variety of methods used to derive an annual count of children in-care. Some jurisdictions do an actual head count on a fixed date. Others report an annual figure that is an average of monthly figures. Still others add the number of children brought into care in a given year to the actual number in care on the first day of the year and subtract the number who left care in the same year. Just to confuse matters even more, some jurisdictions gather and report their data for a fiscal year while others do it on a calendar-year basis. This is an additional limitation to inter-jurisdictional comparisons.

These limitations are compounded by the lack of comprehensive, reliable statistics on Native people, in general, and on children, in particular. We do know that in 1980 there were 302,749 registered status Indians in Canada of whom 160,135 were 19 years of age or under.[4] We only have a rough idea of the total number of non-status Indians and Métis which the Native Council of Canada suggested was between 750,000 and 1,000,000 in 1979.[5] Finally, the total Inuit population is estimated to be between 22,000 and 25,000.

In virtually all cases, the data supplied concerning non-status Indian and Métis children are estimates. Without a commonly accepted definition of non-status Indian or Métis, the decision to categorize a child as one or the other is entirely subjective. And, some provinces argue, the identification of children as non-status Indian or Métis is potentially discriminatory and should not take place. No province or territory appears to have any moral problem with the identification of status Indian children, however, for whom they receive compensation from the federal government. As a result, statistics on status children in care are undoubtedly the most reliable.

Finally, it is virtually impossible to assess long-term trends. The majority of child welfare departments are developing or have implemented computer-based management information systems. Such systems make it easier to compile data and they improve the likelihood of its reliability. Information that shows a large jump in the number of Native children in care in 1981 in a particular province over figures reported in 1971 may be interpreted in different ways. It may very well mean that the situation has worsened — or, it may be that we simply have a more accurate picture of the situation now than in the past.

Given these limitations, the statistics will be presented for each of the provinces and territories with some discussion. Every effort has been made to report figures exactly as they were provided by each jurisdiction. This means that some tables report data on a fiscal year basis, while others will refer to a calendar year. While this may cause some confusion for the reader, it was felt to be the only way to ensure that the information provided by each jurisdiction was reported as accurately as posible. Several tables have also been compiled in an attempt to view the data from a national perspective. In most cases, the data covers the period between 1976 and 1981.

British Columbia

The proportion of Native children in care in British Columbia as shown in Table 1 did not vary substantially during the five-year period 1976-77 to 1980-81. Although there was a decrease of 2 percent from 38.8 to 36.7 percent between 1979-80 and 1980-81, it is impossible to tell whether or not that trend will continue.

The children-in-care count does not include new-born infants placed immediately for adoption, nor does it usually include older children requiring less that seven days care. Children are classified as Native if the racial origin of either parent is given as Native.

The proportion of Native children in foster homes (42.7 percent in 1980-81—see Table 2) is somewhat greater than their proportion of the total in care population as indicated in Table 1 (36.7 percent in 1980-81). Ministry of Human Resources officials estimate that about one-third of those Native children are in Native foster homes.[6]

It appears, however, that Native children are less likely to be placed

TABLE 1
Native Children in Care as a Percentage of All Children in Care of British Columbia's Ministry of Human Resources [a]

Year[b]	Status Indian Children in Care	Non-Status Indian & Métis Children in Care	Total Native Children in Care	Total All Children in Care	Native Children as a % of All Children in Care
1976-77	1,733[c]	1,312[c]	3,045	8,064	37.8
1977-78	1,774	1,177	2,951	7,659	38.5
1978-79	1,692	1,208	2,900	7,396	39.2
1979-80	1,686	1,198	2,884	7,424	38.8
1980-81	1,555	1,119	2,674	7,288	36.7

Source: British Columbia Ministry of Human Resources.
Notes: [a]Figures *do not* include City of Vancouver.
[b]As of last day of fiscal year, March 31.
[c]Estimate.

TABLE 2
Native Children In Foster Homes as a Percentage of All Children in Foster Homes in British Columbia[a]

Year[b]	Total All Children in foster Homes	Total Native Children in Foster Homes	Native Children as a % of All Children in Foster Homes
1978-79	4,670	2,078	44.5
1980-81	4,410[c]	1,884	42.7

Source: British Columbia Ministry of Human Resources.
Notes: [a]Figures *do not* include City of Vancouver.
[b]As of last day of fiscal year, March 31.
[c]Change of method of payment of high "special rates" changed homes serving this type of child to "Special Care Homes" rather than "foster homes" designation.

TABLE 3
Native Children Placed for Adoption as a Percentage of
All Children Placed for Adoption in British Columbia[a]

Year[b]	Total All Children Placed for Adoption	Total Native Children Placed for Adoption[c]	Native Children as a % of All Children Placed for Adoption
1976-77	865	247	28.6
1977-78	654	169	25.8
1978-79	720	189	26.3

Source: British Columbia Ministry of Human Resources.
Notes: [a]Figures *do not* include City of Vancouver.
[b]As of last day of fiscal year, March 31.
[c]These figures do not necessarily appear in the "children-in-care" count in Table 1.

for adoption than non-Native children. Table 3 indicates the proportion of Native children placed for adoption is smaller (26.3 percent in 1978-79) than their proportion of the in care population (39.2 percent in 1978-79).

The British Columbia data is limited because it does not include the city of Vancouver. Ministry officials explained that Vancouver is served by a separate computer system that did not have comparable data available. It is impossible to know what would happen to the percentages if Vancouver were included. Slightly more than 40 percent of status Indian children live off-reserve in British Columbia, a greater proportion than in any other jurisdiction, and it is reasonable to assume that a certain number have gravitated to Vancouver (see Table 33). This suggests that the inclusion of Vancouver statistics may very well increase the percentage of Native children in care.

Alberta

Alberta's Department of Social Services and Community Health provided a detailed breakdown of the number of Native children estimated to be in care of its child welfare department (Tables 4 - 10). Alberta's child welfare program differs to some extent from many other provinces and is an example of the difficulties that arise when interprovincial comparisons are made. Some explanation of the Alberta figures is required so that they can be more fairly compared with other provinces and, especially, in order for the estimate of Native children in care to be accurate and comparable to other provinces.

As previously mentioned, the term "children in care" can sometimes be misleading, and this is especially true in the case of Alberta. In fact, many children receiving assistance in Alberta and included in the children-in-care population are not physically in care.

The total number of children and an estimate of the number of Native children receiving services from Alberta's child welfare department between 1979 and 1981 are provided in Tables 4-6.[7] A breakdown into such categories as permanent wards, custody by agreement, et cetera, appears in these tables. As can be seen from the totals in each table, the estimated proportion of Native children in care is 29.6 percent in 1979, 29.7 percent in 1980, and 28.7 percent in 1981. There are two categories of services, however, that involve a significant number of children and aren't usually included in the child welfare statistics of other provinces.

Some children included in the in-care population are those who committed an offense and are on probation in the care of their parents. A much larger number than these are the physically or mentally disabled. They and their parents receive assistance to minimize the effects of the disability. In many cases, the child remains in his own home, and in all cases, the parents retain full guardianship. In other provinces, children in these categories are not normally counted as part of the in-care population. This is one of the reasons that the number of children in care in Alberta appears to be proportionally larger than in other provinces.

If those categories and the small number of children whose status is unknown are excluded from the in-care count, the total changes significantly and is then more comparable to other provinces. In each instance, the total in-care population would drop from approximately 11,000 to approximately 7,000. The exact numbers are reported in the subtotal in Tables 4-6.

Of particular importance, the proportion of Native children estimated to be in-care changes with the exclusion of these categories. Those estimates, also listed in the subtotals in Tables 4-6, would vary from 44.3 percent in 1979, to 43.7 percent in 1980, to 41.6 percent in 1981. They are a more accurate estimate of the number of Native children in Alberta receiving provincial child welfare services comparable to those provided and reported by other provinces.

In addition, some status Indian children in Alberta are in the direct

TABLE 4

**Native Children in Care as a Percentage of All Children in Care
of Alberta's Department of Social Services and Community Health (Child Welfare), 1979** [a]

Legal Status of Children in Care[b]	Status Indian Children in Care	Non-Status Indian Children in Care	Métis Children in Care	Inuit Children in Care	Total Native Children in Care	Total All Children in Care	Native Children as a % of All Children in Care
Temporary Ward, Child Welfare Act	918	37	730	5	1,690	3,291	51.4
Permanent Ward, Child Welfare Act	431	32	545	8	1,016	2,288	44.4
Custody by Agreement	64	0	52	0	116	556	20.9
Out of Province	15	14	24	2	55	230	23.9
Temporary Ward, Juvenile Delinquent Act	70	2	84	0	156	479	32.6
SUBTOTAL[c]	1,498	85	1,435	15	3,033	6,844	44.3
Probation	72	4	62	0	138	1,200	11.5
Handicapped Children's Services	39	9	59	0	107	3,054	3.5
Status Unknown	0	0	5	0	5	7	71.4
TOTAL	1,609	98	1,561	15	3,283	11,105	29.6

Source: Alberta Department of Social Services and Community Health.
Notes: [a] All figures are estimates based on an average of monthly statistics for calendar year. [b] For a definition of each category see footnote on page 33. [c] See discussion in text.

TABLE 5

**Native Children in Care as a Percentage of All Children in Care
of Alberta's Department of Social Services and Community Health (Child Welfare), 1980[a]**

Legal Status of Children in Care [b]	Status Indian Children in Care	Non-Status Indian Children in Care	Métis Children in Care	Inuit Children in Care	Total Native Children in Care	Total All Children in Care	Native Children as a % of All Children in Care
Temporary Ward, Child Welfare Act	895	24	719	7	1,645	3,298	49.8
Permanent Ward, Child Welfare Act	447	29	542	9	1,027	2,380	43.2
Custody by Agreement	39	0	35	0	74	390	19.0
Out of Province	17	11	20	3	51	229	22.3
Temporary Ward, Juvenile Delinquent Act	63	1	82	0	146	443	33.0
SUBTOTAL[c]	1,461	65	1,398	19	2,943	6,740	43.7
Probation	59	2	40	0	101	915	11.0
Handicapped Children's Services	42	8	64	0	114	2,963	3.8
Status Unknown	0	0	1	0	1	3	33.3
TOTAL	1,562	75	1,503	19	3,159	10,621	29.7

Source: Alberta Department of Social Services and Community Health.
Notes: [a] All figures are estimates based on an average of monthly statistics for calendar year.
[b] For a definition of each category see footnote on page 33. [c] See discussion in text.

TABLE 6
Native Children in Care as a Percentage of All Children in Care
of Alberta's Department of Social Services and Community Health (Child Welfare), 1981[a]

Legal Status of Children in Care[b]	Status Indian Children in Care	Non-Status Indian Children in Care	Métis Children in Care	Inuit Children in Care	Total Native Children in Care	Total All Children in Care	Native Children as a % of All Children in Care
Temporary Ward, Child Welfare Act	876	23	713	9	1,621	3,526	46.0
Permanent Ward, Child Welfare Act	447	27	522	10	1,006	2,350	42.8
Custody by Agreement	35	1	29	0	65	387	16.8
Out of Province	21	8	18	3	50	242	20.7
Temporary Ward, Juvenile Delinquent Act	65	0	83	0	148	450	32.9
SUBTOTAL[c]	1,444	59	1,365	22	2,890	6,955	41.6
Probation	48	1	36	0	85	838	10.1
Handicapped Children's Services	41	8	59	0	108	2,959	3.6
Status Unknown	0	0	0	0	0	0	0
TOTAL	1,533	68	1,460	22	3,083	10,752	28.7

Source: Alberta Social Services and Community Health.
Notes: [a]All figures are estimates based on an average of monthly statistics for calendar year.
[b]For a definition of each category see footnote on page 33. [c]See discussion in text.

NOTES TO TABLES 4-6

The following definitions describe the legal status of the children in care of Alberta's Department of Social Services and Community Health as listed in Tables 4-6

Temporary Ward, Child Welfare Act
A child whose custody and guardianship have been transferred from his/her parents to the director of child welfare in right of the Crown for a period not exceeding one year, by a judge of juvenile and family court or the Court of Queen's Bench, under the authority of Section 24 of the Child Welfare Act.

Permanent Ward, Child Welfare Act
A child whose guardianship has been permanently transferred to the director of child welfare in right of the Crown, either by a justice of the Court of Queen's Bench, under the authority of Section 26 of the Child Welfare Act, or by the voluntary surrender of same by the parents.

Custody by Agreement
A child whose parents have voluntarily and temporarily relinquished his/her care and custody to the director of child welfare, for a period not exceeding six months. Such agreements are provided under Section 35 of the Child Welfare Act.

Out of Province
A child who is in the care of the director of child welfare, but who is residing in another province.

Temporary Ward, Juvenile Delinquent Act
A child who has been adjudged to have committed a delinquency by a judge of juvenile court, and whom the judge has committed to the custody of the director of child welfare as a temporary ward. This guardianship, which may not exceed 12 months, is under the authority of the federal Juvenile Delinquents Act, Section 20 and Section 78(1) of Alberta's Child Welfare Act.

Probation
A child who has been adjudged to have committed a delinquency by a judge of a juvenile court, and who the judge has released from formal custody, under some condition of supervision, to his/her parents' home. Guardianship is not affected. These dispositions are under the authority of Section 20 of the Juvenile Delinquents Act.

Handicapped Children's Services
A handicapped child who has been assessed by a recognized medical

professional as having a chronic physical disability or disorder and/or mental deficiency/disorder of organic cause may receive, under the authority of Section 35 of the Child Welfare Act, financial support to provide the cost of services that will minimize the effect of the handicap on the child and his/her family. The parents retain full guardianship rights to the child, whether the child resides in the family home or in a facility outside the home.

TABLE 7
Native Children in Care of Alberta's Department of Social Services and Community Health and Canada Department of Indian Affairs as a Percentage of All Children in Care in Alberta

	NATIVE CHILDREN IN CARE		
Year[a]	*Alberta Social Services and Community Health*[b]	*Indian Affairs*	*Total*
1979	3,033	122	3,155
1980	2,943	102	3,045
1981	2,890	74	2,964
	ALL CHILDREN IN CARE		
1979	6,844	122	6,966
1980	6,740	102	6,842
1981	6,955	74	7,029
	Native Children as a % of All Children in Care		
1979	45.3		
1980	44.5		
1981	42.2		

Source: Alberta Department of Social Services and Community Health; Canada Department of Indian Affairs, Social Development Directorate, Headquarters.

Notes: [a]Alberta figures are estimated monthly averages for calendar year. Indian Affairs figures are the actual number in care as of March 31.
[b]From subtotals in Tables 4 to 6. Figures exclude children on probation, those receiving services from the Handicapped Children's Services Program or whose status is unknown.

care of Indian Affairs. Obviously, they must be included in the count. The data in Table 7 provides an estimate of the total number of Native children in Alberta receiving child welfare services from Alberta Social Services and Community Health or Indian Affairs that is comparable to those estimates available in other provinces and territories. The final estimates range from 45.3 percent in 1979, to 44.5 percent in 1980, to 42.2 percent in 1981.[8]

With reference to foster care, Native children represented almost half of all children living in foster homes supervised by Alberta Social Services and Community Health in 1979-81 (see Table 8). Slightly less than one-quarter of all Native foster children live in Native foster homes, however, as indicated in Table 9.

Estimates of the number of active children in Alberta placed with a view for adoption are provided in Table 10. They indicate that the percentage of Native children placed for adoption (13 percent in 1981) is substantially less that the proportion they represent (42.2 percent in 1981) of the total in-care population.

One of the most interesting statistics pertaining to Alberta is contained in Table 31, which details the number of all status Indian

TABLE 8
Native Children in Foster Homes as a Percentage
of All Children in Foster Homes Supervised by
Alberta's Department of Social Services and
Community Health (Child Welfare)

Year [a]	Status Indian	Non-Status Indian	Métis	Inuit
1979	1,125	55	1,021	14
1980	1,098	43	1,011	15
1981	1,085	41	993	17

Year [a]	Total Native Children in Foster Homes	Total All Children in Foster Homes	Native Children as % of All Children in Foster Homes
1979	2,215	4,212	52.6
1980	2,167	4,160	52.1
1981	2,136	4,290	49.8

Source: Alberta Department of Social Services and Community Health.
Notes: [a] All figures are estimates based on an average of monthly statistics for calendar year.

35

TABLE 9
Placement of Native Children in Native and Non-Native Foster Homes Supervised by Alberta's Department of Social Services and Community Health (Child Welfare), 1981[a]

Placement	NATIVE FOSTER CHILDREN	
	Number	Percentage
In Native Foster Homes	435	21.7
In Non-Native Foster Homes	1,567	78.3
TOTAL	2,002	100.0

Source: Alberta Department of Social Services and Community Health.
Note: [a]As of March 1981.

TABLE 10
Native Children Placed with a View to Adoption as a Percentage of All Children Placed with a View to Adoption by Alberta's Department of Social Services and Community Health (Child Welfare)

Year[a]	Status Indian	Non-Status Indian	Métis	Inuit
1979	43	9	59	0
1980	38	6	54	1
1981	35	3	44	1

Year[a]	Total Native Children Placed for Adoption	Total All Children Placed for Adoption	Native Children as % of All Children Placed for Adoption
1979	111	639	17.4
1980	99	678	14.6
1981	83	628	13.2

Source: Alberta Department of Social Services and Community Health.
Note: [a]All figures are estimates based on an average of monthly statistics for calendar year.

children in care as a percentage of all status Indian children in each province and territory. Alberta has 7.3 percent, second only to the Yukon at 7.7 percent.

Saskatchewan

Unlike other provinces, child welfare services in Saskatchewan are delivered by two different provincial departments. The operation of child welfare programs in the nothern part of the province is the responsibility of the Department of Northern Saskatchewan.[9] Social Services has jurisdiction in the rest of the province. In addition, a large number of status Indian children are cared for directly by the federal department of Indian Affairs. Table 11 details the total number of Native children in the care of all three departments.

In relation to other provinces and territories, Saskatchewan has one of the highest, if not the highest, proportions of Native children in care. As shown in Table 12, that proportion is estimated to be 62.8 percent in 1976-77, 62.4 percent in percent in 1977-78, 65.0 percent in 1978-79, 66.8 percent in 1979-80,and 63.8 percent in 1980-81.

It must be remembered that the Native population in Saskatchewan is probably higher than in any other province. Table 30, for example, lists the number of status Indian children 0-19 years of age as a proportion of all children 0-19. The Saskatchewan figure of 8.3 percent is exceeded only by the Yukon and Northwest Territories.There exists no hard data on non-status Indian and Métis children. It seems reasonable to assume that they may also represent a larger proportion of the total child population in Saskatchewan than in other provinces. It is improbable, however, that such a figure would even begin to approach the 60-65 percent range that is the proportion of Native children in care.

Saskatchewan does not keep statistics on the placement of Native children in foster homes, although, a one-time count was undertaken by Saskatchewan Social Services in 1981. That survey indicated that 1,201 Native children were living in foster homes.[10] That represents 76.8 percent of the total of 1,567 children placed in foster homes supervised by Saskatchewan Social Services as of 31 March 1981.Of those 1,201 Native foster children, it was determined that 101 were living in 73 Native foster homes. The remaining 91.5 percent were living in non-Native foster homes.

Complete and accurate statistics on the adoption of Native children are not maintained either. Saskatchewan Social Services estimates, however, that about 150, or 37.5 percent of the approximately 400 children placed for adoption each year are Native children. Of those, it is estimated that approximately 20 percent are placed with Native families.[11] These estimates correspond with figures that do exist on the adoption of status Indian children. They are provided in Table 13.

37

TABLE 11
Total Number of Native Children In Care in Saskatchewan

| | SASKATCHEWAN SOCIAL SERVICES [a] | | DEPARTMENT OF NORTHERN SASKATCHEWAN [b] | | INDIAN AFFAIRS [c] | TOTAL NATIVE CHILDREN IN CARE |
	Status Indians	Non-Status Indians & Métis	Status Indians	Non-Status Indians & Métis	Status Indians	
Year						
1976-77	573	577	d	d	679	1,829
1977-78	587	536	d	d	695	1,818
1978-79	696	405	57	95	637	1,890
1979-80	700	413	70	118	577	1,878
1980-81	789	420	66	110	477	1,862

Source: Saskatchewan Social Services; Department of Northern Saskatchewan; Canada Department of Indian Affairs, Social Development Directorate, Headquarters.

Notes: [a]Figures represent total number of children admitted to care by fiscal year.
[b]Figures are estimates.
[c]Figures represent actual number of children in care on last day of fiscal year.
[d]Department of Northern Saskatchewan figures are included with those of Saskatchewan Social Services.

TABLE 12

Native Children in Care of Saskatchewan Social Services, the Department of Northern Saskatchewan and Canada Department of Indian Affairs as a Percentage of All Children in Care in Saskatchewan

	ALL CHILDREN IN CARE					
Year	Saskatchewan Social Services [a]	Department of Northern Saskatchewan [b]	Indian Affairs [c]	Total	Native Children in Care	Native Children as a % of All Children in Care
1976-77	2,234	[d]	679	2,913	1,829	62.8
1977-78	2,218	[d]	695	2,913	1,818	62.4
1978-79	2,099	173	637	2,909	1,890	65.0
1979-80	2,022	214	577	2,813	1,878	66.8
1980-81	2,240	200	477	2,917	1,862	63.8

Source: Saskatchewan Social Services; Department of Northern Saskatchewan; Canada Department of Indian Affairs, Social Development Directorate, Headquarters.

Notes: [a]Figures represent total number of children admitted to care by fiscal year.
[b]Figures are estimates.
[c]Figures represent actual number of children in care on last day of fiscal year.
[d]Department of Northern Saskatchewan figures are included with those of Saskatchewan Social Services.

TABLE 13
Adoption of Status Indian Children in Saskatchewan
by Indian and Non-Indian Families

Year [a]	By Indians	By Non-Indians	Total	% Adopted by Non-Indians
1977	7	71	78	91.0
1978	14	81	95	85.3
1979	20	110	130	84.6
1980	15	68	83	81.9
1981	18	75	93	80.5

Source: Canada Department of Indian Affairs, Social Development Directorate, Headquarters.
Note: [a]Figures are for calendar year.

In 1981, approximately 20 percent of status Indian children who were adopted were placed with Indian families or parents, while 80 percent were placed in non-Indian homes.

Manitoba

It is very difficult to determine the number and proportion of Native children in care in Manitoba. Manitoba's Child Welfare Directorate was unable to provide an estimate of the number of Indian and Métis children in its care. They did provide figures for status Indian children, but even then it was a range of between 600 and 700 per month. Using the midpoint in that range—650—slightly less than one-third of all children in the care of Manitoba's Department of Community Services and Corrections and the federal Department of Indian Affairs are status Indian children. As indicated in Table 14, 29.9 percent of all children in care in 1979-80 and 32.1 percent in 1980-81 are estimated to be status Indian.

Obviously, if non-status Indian and Métis children were included, the proportion of all Native children in care would increase substantially. One previous study estimated that the figure would be 60 percent.[12] Representatives of the provincial Child Welfare Directorate did offer some estimates in 1980. At that time 40 to 50 percent of all children in its care were considered to be of Indian ancestry. The total number of non-status Indian and Métis children

TABLE 14

Status Indian Children in Care of Manitoba's Department of Community Services and Corrections and Canada Department of Indian Affairs as a Percentage of All Children in Care in Manitoba

Year[a]	STATUS INDIAN CHILDREN			ALL CHILDREN			Status Indian Children as a % of All Children in Care
	In Care of Manitoba[b]	In Care of Indian Affairs	Total	In Care of Manitoba	In Care of Indian Affairs	Total	
1979-80	650	484	1,134	3,304	484	3,788	29.9
1980-81	650	531	1,181	3,145	531	3,676	32.1

Source: Manitoba Department of Community Services and Corrections; Canada Department of Indian and Northern Affairs Social Development Directorate Headquarters.

Notes: [a]Number of children in care at fiscal year end, March 31.
[b]The number of status Indian children in care was estimated to average between 600 and 700 per month.

TABLE 15

**Native Children Placed for Adoption as a Percentage of
All Children Placed for Adoption by Manitoba's Department of
Community Services and Corrections, 1981**

Indian Children	Métis Children	Total Native Children	Total All Children	Native Children as a % of All Children Placed for Adoption
112	95	207	425	48.7

Source: Background Information prepared for Kimelman Review Committee on Indian and Métis Adoptions and Placements.

was estimated to be 120,000 or slightly less than three times the 44,500 status Indian children.[13] If the figure of 50 percent is used and the approximately 500 status Indian children in the care of Indian Affairs are included, the estimate of all Native children in care would increase to 56 percent. The only thing that can be said about Manitoba with any certainty is that a highly disproportionate number of children of Indian ancestry are in care.

Some more detailed estimates are starting to emerge in Manitoba as a result of a review of placement procedures involving Native children that began in 1982 and is being conducted by a committee headed by Judge E.C. Kimelman. Table 15 was constructed from information prepared for that review. It indicates that 48.7 percent of all children in Manitoba placed for adoption in 1981 were Indian or Métis. That figure is much higher than the proportion of Native children placed for adoption in other provinces (see Tables 3 and 10, for example). Until 1982, Manitoba was the only jurisdiction in Canada that still placed significant numbers of Native children in the United States. For example, 34 Indian children, or 38 percent of all Indian children adopted in Manitoba in 1981, and 18 Métis children, or 17 percent of all Métis children in Manitoba adopted in that same year, were placed in the U.S.[14] Comparable data on placement in foster and group care were not available.

Ontario

All child welfare services provided to status and non-status Indian and Métis families in Ontario are delivered via a province-wide system of Children's Aid Societies. During the five-year period 1977-81, as shown in Table 16, Native children accounted for approximately 8 percent of all children in care of Children's Aid Societies in each year. In relation to the four western provinces and the two territories, the figure of 8 percent seems low. It is important to remember, however, that Native people represent a much smaller proportion of the total population in Ontario, Quebec and the Atlantic provinces than they do in the western provinces and the territories. Table 30 presents the number of status Indian children 0-19 years as a percentage of all children 0-19 years of age for 1979-80. In Ontario the figure was 1.1 percent. By comparison 8.3 percent of all children in Saskatchewan and 18.7 percent of all children in the Northwest Territories were status Indian.

TABLE 16
Native Children in Care of Ontario's Children's Aid Societies as a Percentage of All Children In Care in Ontario

Year [a]	Total Native Children in Care [b]	Total All Children in Care	Native Children as a % of All Children in Care
1977	1,134	13,131	8.6
1978	1,097	13,814	7.9
1979	1,102	14,008	7.9
1980	1,045	13,033	8.0
1981	998	12,928	7.7

Source: Ontario Ministry of Community and Social Services, Children's Aid Societies Form V Year-End Summaries.
Notes: [a]Figures are for calendar year.
[b]Includes all registered status Indian children living on reserves and those of Indian ancestry who identify with their Indian heritage, including non-status Indian and Métis children.
[c]Total for 1981 is an estimate based on monthly averages from January to September.

TABLE 17
Adoption of Status Indian Children in Ontario by Indian and Non-Indian Families

Year[a]	By Indians	By Non-Indians	Total	% Adopted by Non-Indians
1977	35	48	83	57.8
1978	31	68	99	68.7
1979	28	66	94	70.2
1980	23	63	86	73.3
1981	21	56	77	72.7

Source: Canada Department of Indian Affairs, Social Development Directorate, Headquarters.
Note: [a]Figures are for calendar year.

The proportion of Native children in care in Ontario is small, in other words, because the proporation on Native children as a whole is small. In Ontario's case, this fact is somewhat deceptive because the vast majority of Native people live in northern Ontario. The overall provincial figures mask the fact that Native people are disproportionately represented in northern Ontario Children's Aid Societies.

Although an extreme example, the Kenora CAS is a case in point. In 1981 a Kenora CAS official estimated that approximately 85 percent of children in its care were of Indian ancestry. [15] The proportion of Native children in care of some northern Ontario CASs may be higher than the estimates provided by the four western provinces even though the overall Ontario percentage is lower.

Quebec

Child welfare services are delivered to the majority of status Indians living on reserves in Quebec by agreement with local social service centres. The numbers receiving service are listed in Table 18. In addition, Quebec's Ministry of Social Affairs gradually began to assume responsibility for providing child welfare services to the Cree and Inuit living in the James Bay area as a result of the James Bay Agreement, ratified in 1975. During that period the number of Cree and Inuit began to be reported separately — as reflected in Table 18.

44

TABLE 18

**Status Indian, Cree and Inuit Children in Care as a Percentage of
All Children in Care of Quebec's Ministry of Social Affairs**

Year	Status Indian	Cree	Inuit
1977-78	482	b	b
1978-79	590	b	12
1979-80	592	38	8
1980-81	594	41	15
1981-82	623	52	16

Year	Total Status Indian, Cree and Inuit in Care	Total All Children in Care[a]	Status Indian, Cree and Inuit Children as a % of All Children in Care
1977-78	482	29,259	1.6
1978-79	602	28,870	2.1
1979-80	638	27,136	2.4
1980-81	650	24,884	2.6
1981-82	691	n/a	n/a

Source: Quebec Ministry of Social Affairs.
Notes: [a]Figures for the total number of children in care as of November of that fiscal year.
[b]Responsibility for health and social services for the James Bay Cree and Inuit began to be transferred to Quebec after the signing of the James Bay Agreement in 1975. The transfer was completed as of March 31 1981.

The total proportion of Native children in care appears to be relatively small, but status Indian children living off-reserve, as well as non-status Indian and Métis children, are not included in that count. Nevertheless, the five-year period 1977-78 to 1981-82 witnessed an absolute increase of approximately 200 status Indian, Cree and Inuit children in care. As a result, their representation in the total in-care count increased from 1.6 to 2.6 percent in a four-year period.

The inclusion of non-status Indian and Métis children, as well as off-reserve status Indian children, would undoubtedly increase that percentage, although it is difficult to determine by how much. It is interesting to note that approximately 4.0 percent of all status Indian children in Quebec are in care, which is about double the figure of 2.2 percent in Ontario (see Table 31). This difference may be explained, however, by the fact that the total number of children included in the in-care figure in Quebec is about twice that of Ontario's, even though the child population is smaller in absolute terms.

Native children in Quebec are much more likely to be placed in Native foster homes than they are in many other provinces. The statistics presented in Table 19 show that about one-half of all status

TABLE 19
Placement of Status Indian, Cree and Inuit Children in
Native and Non-Native Foster Homes Authorized by
Quebec's Ministry of Social Affairs

	Year	In Native Foster Home	In Non-Native Foster Home
Status	1977-78	229	228
Indian	1978-79	290	272
	1979-80	294	268
Cree	1979-80	38	0
	1980-81	39	2
	1981-82	50	2
Inuit	1978-79	12	0
	1979-80	7	1
	1980-81	14	1
	1981-82	16	0

Source: Quebec Ministry of Social Affairs.

TABLE 20
Native Foster Homes in Quebec

Year	Number
1977-78	183
1978-79	232
1979-80	235
1980-81	240
1981-82	249

Source: Quebec Ministry of Social Affairs.

TABLE 21
Adoption of Status Indian, Cree and Inuit Children in
Quebec by Native and Non-Native Families

	Year	By Native Families	By Non-Native Families
Status	1977-78	9	3
Indian	1978-79	10	3
	1979-80	10	4
	1980-81	16	6
	1981-82	12	5
Cree	1978-79	21	0
	1979-80	17	1
	1980-81	29	0
	1981-82	19	0
Inuit	1978-79	19	1
	1979-80	14	0
	1980-81	21	0
	1981-82	16	0

Source: Quebec Ministry of Social Affairs.

Indian foster children are in foster homes operated by someone of Indian ancestry. There are in excess of 200 such homes, as shown in Table 20. Virtually all Cree and Inuit children are in Native foster homes, which in all probability are in their own communities.

That situation is true, as well, in the case of adoption (see Table 21). Although the total number of status Indian children placed for adoption is relatively small, the majority of them have been placed with Indian families. Only one Cree and one Inuit child were placed for adoption with a non-Native family between 1978-79 and 1981-82. This reflects the prevalence and provincial acceptance of the practice of custom adoption (the raising of a child by relatives other than the parents), which has been an integral feature of Cree and Inuit life.

New Brunswick

The total number of Native children in care (81 in 1980-81) is relatively small, as is their proportion (3.9 percent in 1980-81) of the total in-care population (Table 22). It should be pointed out, however, that the figures given refer only to status Indians. They do not include non-status Indian or Métis children. As of September 1981, New Brunswick officials estimated that 63 Indian children were living in Native foster homes and 28 in non-Native homes.[16]

TABLE 22
Status Indian Children in Care as a Percentage of All Children in Care of New Brunswick's Department of Social Services

Year[a]	Status Indian Children in Care	All Children in Care	Status Indian Children as a % of All Children in Care
1978-79	80[b]	2,270	3.5
1979-80	75[b]	2,059	3.6
1980-81	81	2,028	3.9

Source: New Brunswick Department of Social Services.
Notes: [a]In-care population on last day of fiscal year, March 31.
[b]Estimate.

Nova Scotia

The actual numbers of Native children in care in Nova Scotia approximate those reported for New Brunswick, although the proportion they represent of all children in care (4.3 percent in 1980-81) is slightly higher (Table 23). It is believed that the figures for Nova Scotia refer only to status Indian children and do not include non-status Indian or Métis children. The statistics reported by Nova Scotia officials also indicate that very few Indian children are placed with non-Native foster or adoptive families. Of the eight status Indian children in Nova Scotia who were placed for adoption in 1980-81, for example, six were adopted by Indian families and only two by non-Indian families.[17]

48

TABLE 23
Status Indian Children in Care as a Percentage of All Children in Care of Nova Scotia's Department of Social Services

Year[a]	Status Indian Children in Care	All Children in Care	Status Indian Children as a % of All Children in Care
1978-79	81	1,959	4.1
1979-80	97	1,840	5.3
1980-81	76	1,759	4.3

Source: Nova Scotia Department of Social Services.
Note: [a]In-care population on last day of fiscal year, March 31.

Prince Edward Island

The number of Native children in care reported by Prince Edward Island for the year 1981 (Table 24) was relatively small, but of particular interest precisely for that reason.

As of September 1981, P.E.I.'s Department of Health and Social Services had 233 children in its care — 25, or 10.7 percent, of whom were either status or non-status Indians. It seems logical to suggest that because the total number is very small, P.E.I.'s estimate of the status and non-status Indian children in its care may be among the

TABLE 24
Native Children in Care as a Percentage of All Children in Care of Prince Edward Island's Department of Health and Social Services

Year[a]	Status Indian Children in Care	Non-Status Indian Children in Care	Total Native Children in Care	Total All Children in Care	Native Children as a % of All Children in Care
1981	14	11	25	233	10.7

Source: Prince Edward Island Department of Health and Social Services.
Note: [a]Total in-care population as of September.

most accurate of any province. If this is true, the actual proportion of all Native children in care may be significantly higher in Nova Scotia and New Brunswick than indicated by the estimates in Tables 22-23, which do not include non-status Indian children.

TABLE 25
Native Children in Care of Newfoundland and Labrador's Department of Social Services

Year	Native Children in Care	All Children in Care
1976-77	108[a]	1,383
1977-78	108[a]	1,274
1978-79	108[a]	1,221
1979-80	108[a]	1,263
1980-81	108[a]	1,276

Source: Newfoundland and Labrador Department of Social Services Division of Child Welfare.
Notes: [a]The number of Native children estimated to be in care is a cumulative number over the period 1976-81 rather than a yearly count.

Newfoundland and Labrador

The statistics provided by Newfoundland and Labrador were cumulative totals for a five-year period from 1976 to 1981 rather than a yearly count. As indicated in Table 25, it was estimated that 108 Native children had come into care during that period. The total number of children in care in each of those years was approximately 1,300

During that same period, 27 Native children were placed in Native foster homes and 45 with non-Native foster families. Five Native children were adopted by Native families and three by non-Native families.

Of the 108 Native children in care, 53 were permanent wards, 43 temporary wards, eight non-wards and two status unknown. Thirty-seven were discharged from care and returned to their parents.[18]

Northwest Territories

Statistics on the number of Native children in care in the Northwest Territories are of particular interest because of the relatively large Native population there. Table 26 presents a very rough estimate of the

50

TABLE 26

Native Children in Care as a Percentage of All Children in Care of the Northwest Territories' Department of Social Services

Year [a]	Déné-Status Indians	Métis	Inuit	Total Native Children in Care [b]	Total All Children in Care [c]	Native Children in Care as a % of All Children in Care
1980	71	48	56	175	368	47.5

Source: Northwest Territories Department of Social Services.
Notes: [a] As of December 31.
[b] Very rough estimate.
[c] Includes those admitted under the Child Welfare Ordinance, the Juvenile Delinquents Act, and parental agreement.

number and proportion of Native children in care. In 1980 it was estimated that slightly less than half, or 47.5 percent, of all children in care were Déné Indian, Métis or Inuit.

A detailed description of the placement of Native children in foster homes is presented in Table 27. Approximately 25 percent or 35 of the 139 Native children placed in foster homes in 1980 were placed outside of the Northwest Territories. None were placed outside of Canada, however.

A majority of all Native foster children from the Northwest Territories were placed in non-Native foster homes. Of the Déné children, 35 (or 57.4 percent) were placed in non-Native settings. The proportion was almost the same for Métis children at 57.1 percent or 16 children. Exactly 74 percent or 37 of the 50 Inuit foster children were placed with non-Native foster families.

Table 28 presents data on adoption placements of children from the Northwest Territories and is indicative of the prevalence of the practice of custom adoption. In 1980, 45.1 percent of all adoptions in the Northwest Territories were custom adoptions. In 1981, that figure was 51.2 percent.

TABLE 27
Placement of Déné-Status Indian, Métis and Inuit Children in Foster Homes Supervised by the Northwest Territories' Department of Social Services, 1980

		TOTAL
DÉNÉ STATUS INDIAN FOSTER CHILDREN		
Placed in the Northwest Territories		
• In Déné homes	21	
• In non-Native homes	23	
• In Métis homes	4	
SUBTOTAL	48	48
Placed outside of the Northwest Territories		
• In non-Native homes	12	
• In Métis homes	1	
SUBTOTAL	13	13
TOTAL DÉNÉ FOSTER CHILDREN		61
MÉTIS FOSTER CHILDREN		
Placed in the Northwest Territories		
• In non-Native homes	10	
• In Métis homes	11	
SUBTOTAL	21	21
Placed outside of the Northwest Territories		
• In non-Native homes	6	
• In Métis homes	1	
SUBTOTAL	7	7
TOTAL MÉTIS FOSTER CHILDREN		28
INUIT FOSTER CHILDREN		
Placed in the Northwest Territories		
• In non-Native homes	23	
• In Inuit homes	12	
SUBTOTAL	35	35
Place outside of the Northwest Territories		
• In non-Native homes	14	
• In Métis homes	1	
SUBTOTAL	15	15
TOTAL INUIT FOSTER CHILDREN		50
TOTAL—ALL NATIVE FOSTER CHILDREN		139

Source: Northwest Territories Department of Social Services.

TABLE 28
Native Custom Adoptions as a Percentage of All Adoptions
Authorized by the Northwest Territories' Department of
Social Services

Year	Total Custom Adoptions	Total All Adoptions	Custom Adoptions as a % of All Adoptions
1980	60	133	45.1
1981	42	82	51.2

Source: Northwest Territories Department of Social Services.

Yukon Territory

The data provided by the Yukon refer only to status Indian children (Table 29). They indicate that in each year from 1976 to 1981 more than half of all children in the care of the Yukon's Department of Health and Human Resources were status Indian. The percentages during that period range form a low of 54.5 percent in 1977-78 to a high of 65.8 percent in 1979-1980.

TABLE 29
Status Indian Children in Care as a Percentage
of All Children in Care of the Yukon's Department
of Health and Human Resources

Year[a]	Status Indian Children in Care	All Children in Care	Status Indian Children as a % of All Children in Care
1976-77	119[b]	194	61.3
1977-78	103	189	54.5
1978-79	109	194	56.2
1979-80	104	158	65.8
1980-81	82	134	61.2

Source: Yukon Department of Health & Human Resources.
Notes: [a] As of last day of fiscal year, March 31.
[b] In 1977 an additional 19 status Indian Children were in the direct care of Indian Affairs.

53

It is important to remember, however, that the Yukon has a relatively large number of status Indian children compared with its total child population. In 1979-80, 16.4 percent of all Yukon children were status Indians, making the Yukon second only to the Northwest Territories in having the largest proportion of status Indian children (see Table 30). Nevertheless, as in most other jurisdictions in Canada, the proportion of status Indian children in care in the Yukon was significantly higher than their proportion of the total child population.

Statistics on the number of Native children in foster homes were not available. Yukon officials did undertake a survey in October 1980, however, which indicated that exactly 50 percent of all existing approved foster and group homes had either one or both parents who were of Indian ancestry.[19]

The National Picture

As difficult as it is to make inter-provincial/territorial comparisons, the data contained here suggests a number of themes common to most jurisdictions. Most of the following tables allow for jurisdictional comparisons of status Indian children. Statistics on status Indian children are more reliable than those on the other segments of the Native child population. Not only is there a legal definition of them, but there is a central data collection point in the Social Development Directorate of Indian Affairs in Ottawa. An analysis of the data on status Indian children allows us to make slightly better informed assumptions about non-status Indian and Métis children.

The tables make it very obvious that the issue of child welfare and Native Peoples is of particular concern in northern Ontario, the four western provinces, and the two territories. The number of Native children involved in the child welfare systems in all of these jurisdictions is large both absolute and relative terms. This is not particularly surprising, since the Native population is largest in these areas. Table 30 presents data on the number of status Indian children 0-19 years of age as a proportion of all children that age in each province and territory. Not surprisingly, the proportion of status Indian children is largest in the two territories, followed by Saskatchewan, Manitoba, British Columbia and Alberta, in that order. There is a marked difference east of the Manitoba border, with the proportion of status Indian children averaging slightly less than 1 percent. If accurate statistics on non-status Indian and Métis children were available, they would undoubtedly show a similar pattern. To some

TABLE 30
Status Indian Children as a Percentage of All Children in Canada 0-19 Years of Age, 1979-80

Province/Territory	All Children 0-19 yrs [a]	Status Indian Children 0-19 yrs [b]	Status Indian Children as a % of All Children
Newfoundland	238,900	0	0
P.E.I.	44,700	251	0.6
Nova Scotia	291,200	2,611	0.9
New Brunswick	252,900	2,500	1.0
Quebec	2,030,400	14,943	.7
Ontario	2,747,800	30,595	1.1
Manitoba	341,900	26,178	7.7
Saskatchewan	337,200	27,886	8.3
Alberta	729,300	21,491	2.9
British Columbia	821,000	28,400	3.5
Yukon	8,200	1,344	16.4
N.W.T.	21,000	3,936	18.7
CANADA	7,864,500	160,135	2.0

Source: Indian and Northern Affairs; Statistics Canada, Demography Division.
Notes: [a] Final postcensal estimate as of 1 June 1980.
[b] As of 31 December 1979.

extent, this explains the large number of Native children in care in the western provinces and in the territories. But while this is more of a "western" and "northern" issue, Table 31 makes it clear that the problem is nationwide.

The information in Table 31 tallies the total number of status Indian children in each province/territory who are in the care of provincial/territorial child welfare departments and/or Indian Affairs. The last column presents that number as a proportion of all status Indian children. The statistics indicate that even in parts of the country where the actual number of status Indian children in care is relatively small, they still represent a significant proportion of all status Indian children.

TABLE 31
Status Indian Children in Care in Canada as a Percentage of
All Status Indian Children, 1979-80

Province/Territory	All Status Indian Children 0-19 yrs.[a]	Status Indian Children in Care of Province/Territory[b]	Status Indian Children in Care of Indian Affairs	Total All Status Indian Children in Care	Status Indian Children in Care as a % of All Status Children 0-19yrs.
Atlantic	5,362	172	33	205	3.8
Quebec	14,943	592	4	596	4.0
Ontario	30,595	658	0	658	2.2
Manitoba	26,178	650[c]	484	1,134	4.3
Saskatchewan	27,886	770	577	1,347	4.8
Alberta	21,491	1,461	102	1,563	7.3
British Columbia	28,400	1,686	0	1,686	5.9
Yukon Territory	1,344	104[c]	0	104	7.7
N.W.T.	3,936	71	0	71	1.8
CANADA	160,135	6,164	1,200	7,364	4.6

Source: Canada Department of Indian and Northern Affairs, Social Development Directorate, Headquarters; provincial and territorial governments.

Notes: [a] As of 31 December 1979
[b] As of 31 March 1980.
[c] Estimate.

As of 1 June 1980, it was estimated that there were 7,864,500 children in Canada 0-19 years of age.[20] As of 31 March 1980, approximately 75,000 children were estimated to be in care in Canada.[21] In comparison with the data compiled for this book, that estimate seems to be fairly high. Nevertheless, it indicates that .96 percent of all children in Canada were in the care of child welfare authorities in 1980. Table 31 demonstrates, however, that 4.6 percent of all status Indian children were in care. In other words, status Indian children were represented in the child welfare system at approximately four and a half times the rate for all children in Canada. There is every reason to believe that the same is true for non-status Indian and Métis children. Quite clearly, it is a national problem.

It has been alleged in the past that when placed in foster homes, Native children are much more likely to be placed with non-Native foster families. The evidence presented in these tables clearly confirms that belief.

The statistics also verify that Native children are less likely to be placed for adoption than non-Native children. That in itself may not be

TABLE 32
Adoption of Status Indian Children by Indian
and Non-Indian Families-Canada

Year [a]	By Indians	By Non-Indians	Total	% Adopted By Non-Indians
1971	45	235	280	83.9
1972	48	269	317	84.9
1973	100	328	428	76.6
1974	104	261	365	71.5
1975	99	247	346	71.4
1976	114	381	495	77.0
1977	127	385	512	75.1
1978	111	354	465	76.1
1979	156	433	589	73.5
1980	131	435	566	76.8
1981	118	401	519	77.2

Source: Canada Department of Indian and Northern Affairs, Social Development Directorate.
Note: [a]Figures are for calendar year.

TABLE 33
Status Indian Children Living Off-Reserve
as a Percentage of All Status Indian Children
in Canada, 1979 [a]

Province/Territory	All Status Indian Children 0-19 yrs.	Status Indian Children 0-19 yrs. living On-Reserve [b]	Status Indian Children 0-19 yrs. living Off-Reserve	Status Indian Children Living Off-Reserve as a % of All Status Indian Children
P.E.I.	251	173	78	31.0
Nova Scotia	2,611	2,123	488	18.7
New Brunswick	2,500	2,052	448	17.9
Quebec	14,943	13,337	1,606	10.7
Ontario	30,595	21,888	8,707	28.5
Manitoba	26,178	19,032	7,146	27.3
Saskatchewan	27,886	18,141	9,745	34.9
Alberta	21,491	16,273	5,218	24.3
British Columbia	28,400	16,929	11,471	40.4
N.W.T.	3,936	3,680	256	6.5
Yukon	1,344	1,028	316	23.5
CANADA	160,135	114,656	45,479	28.4

Source: Indian and Northern Affairs.
Notes: [a] All figures are as of 31 December 1979.
[b] Including those living on Crown land.

a bad thing, if the only alternative is to increase the placement of Native children for adoption in non-Native homes or, even worse, in homes outside the country. It may mean, though, that Native children are more likely to get "stuck" in the system and stay in group homes or institutions, which may be no more appropriate.

Certainly, the available data demonstrates that status Indian children placed for adoption are still much more likely to be adopted by non-Indian families. Table 32 (on page 57) presents national figures on the adoption placement of status Indian children during the ten-year period 1971-81. The proportion of status Indian children adopted by non-Indians during that period ranged from a high of 84.9 percent in 1972 to a low of 71.4 percent in 1975. During the five years from 1977 to 1981, that figure was consistently in the 75 percent range.

The final piece of information of particular significance is contained in Table 33. As of 31 December 1979, 28.4 percent of all status Indian children in Canada between the ages of 0 and 19 were living off-reserve. A large number of them would have been living in urban centres. The phenomenon of the urban Indian child is of tremendous importance for child welfare planners and practitioners in urban areas. It should be of special interest to those living in provinces where the percentage of status Indian children living off-reserve is much higher than the national average.

THE HUMAN TOLL

The sea of statistics detailed in this chapter is useful, but it can mask the effects the Sixties Scoop has had on individual children, families and communities.

Many experts in the child welfare field are coming to believe that the removal of any child from his/her parents is inherently damaging, in and of itself. Dr. Chris Bagley, Burns professor of child welfare at the University of Calgary, said, "In our opinion ... separation from parents — even from supposedly 'bad' or 'abusing' parents — has profound, negative and sometimes disastrous psychological consequences for a child."[22] If his thesis is correct, more damage will have been done to Native children as a whole because a disproportionately larger number of them have been removed from their parents and families.

The effects of apprehension on an individual Native child will often be much more traumatic than for his non-Native counterpart. Frequently, when the Native child is taken from his parents, he is also removed from a tightly knit community of extended family members and neighbours, who may have provided some support. In addition, he is removed from a unique, distinctive and familiar culture. The Native child is placed in a position of triple jeopardy. This multiple blow to Native children who are apprehended was recognized by Alberta's Ombudsman in a 1981 investigation into the foster care program in that province.[23] The damage done is even acknowledged by federal officials, at least in private. An early draft of memorandum prepared for Cabinet that outlined the details of the Canada-Manitoba-Indian Child Welfare Agreement stated that

> many Indian children have been lost to their families and bands and have suffered serious cultural conflicts arising from their placement in foster homes and institutions alien to their social and cultural experience and from adoption by non-Indians.[24]

That excerpt perfectly describes the experience of 15 year-old Garry, who in 1982 was living in a group home in one of the territories.[25] At the age of three, Garry, an Indian, was placed with a foster family after the death of both his parents. The foster family was not Indian. Moreover, they openly disparaged and criticized Indians.

Garry lived with this foster family for many years and grew up thinking that all Indians were lazy, drunken and "good for nothing." As he matured, he gradually became aware that he was somehow different from his foster family. He looked more like those people his foster parents said were lazy, drunken and "good for nothing." Eventually, Garry came to understand that he was Indian.

Not suprisingly, after ten years the relationship between Garry and his foster parents began to deteriorate. Garry started to get into trouble. Finally, the placement broke down completely and Garry was moved to a group home. Garry's experience with the child welfare system is not that uncommon, and variations of his story can be told by countless other Native people.

The effects of apprehension are often as painful for the parents as they are for the child. This may be particularly true for Native families, who, if anything, are more child-centred than many non-Native families. Often, difficulties they may have been experiencing are further aggravated. Problems of alcoholism and emotional stress can be exacerbated when a child is removed, which, in turn, increases the likelihood of other children being apprehended.[26] For many Native parents who already have low self-esteem, the removal of a child is but another confirmation of their feeling of worthlessness.

One Indian parent who experienced the agony of seeing his children removed is now chief of the Big Grassy Reserve in northwestern Ontario. Moses Tom described his feeling of powerlessness when four of his eight children were apprehended by the Children's Aid Society at a period in his life when he was having severe alcohol problems.[27] The courtroom procedures were extremely bewildering, and he was unable to understand much of what went on because his knowledge of English was minimal.

Not only were his children removed, some were quite literally lost to him. Two were sent to the United Kingdom, and Tom and his wife have never seen them again. The other two were placed in adoption homes that weren't successful and have since been in and out of institutions for emotionally disturbed children.

Chief Tom eventually resolved his drinking problem and saw the four children who were not taken from him all go on to attend university and college. Even the current director of the local CAS questions past practices. In commenting on the experience of Chief Tom, he said, "When you see this, you've got to wonder about what we've been doing." [28] The ultimate irony of Moses Tom's story is that he now works part-time as a child welfare worker for the Rainy River CAS.

The disproportionately high number of Native children removed during the Sixties Scoop has also inflicted severe damage on Native culture and society as a whole. The family was and still is central to Native life. In the words of the Indian Homemakers' Association of British Columbia:

> While the family is said to be the base of any society, the family for Indian people is of still greater importance. It is the very foundation of our culture. In contrast to the individualistic, nuclear family concept of the non-Indian people we are culturally a communal society which functions within the framework of the extended family.[29]

The apprehension of Native children weakens Native families and, in so doing, weakens Native society as a whole.

Some Native Peoples go even further and argue that existing child welfare practices threaten the very existence and survival of a unique, distinct Native culture. The British Columbia Native Women's Society, for example, refers to the United Nation's definition of genocide to support this argument.[30] Acts of genocide include forcibly transferring the children of one group to another group. The key to the UN definition is that such transfers are done with the intention of destroying a culture. Canada's systems of child welfare have effectively transferred large numbers of Native children to another, non-Native, group. And, while it may be true that this was not done with the intent of destroying Native culture, the effects are the same. Arguments like those of the B.C. Native Women's Society cannot be easily dismissed.

In retrospect, the wholesale apprehension of Native children during the Sixties Scoop appears to have been a terrible mistake. While some individual children may have benefitted, many did not. Nor did their families. And Native culture suffered one of many severe blows. Unfortunately, the damage is still being done. While attitudes may have changed to some extent since the Sixties, Native children continue to be represented in the child welfare system at a much greater rate than non-Native children. The reasons will be discussed in the next chapter.

Notes to Chapter 2

[1] John A. MacDonald, *"The Spallumcheen Indian Band By-Law and Its Potential Impact on Native Indian Child Welfare Policy in British Columbia"* (Vancouver: School of Social Work, University University of British Columbia, April 1981), pp. 6-7.

[2] In conversation with the author, September 1981.

[3] See for example, Pete Hudson and Brad McKenzie, "Child Welfare and Native Peoples: The Extension of Colonialism," *Social Worker*, vol. 49, no. 2 (Summer 1981).

[4] Canada, Department of Indian and Northern Affairs.

[5] Harry W. Daniels, ed.,*The Forgotten People* (Ottawa: Native Council of Canada, 1979), p. 1.

[6] Correspondence from David S. S. Marshall,British Columbia Ministry of Human Resources, 23 October 1981.

[7] These figures *do not* include other categories of service, such as family support and supervision orders. Family support services, which provide at-home services to families with children, would increase the total number of children served by 2,142 in 1979, 2,850 in 1980, and 2,787 in 1981. The proportion of Native children to all children receiving such services was estimated to be 28.2 percent in 1979, 26.0 percent in 1980, and 21.0 percent in 1981.

[8] These figures are in keeping with the estimate of 45 percent provided by Alberta's Office of the Ombudsman, "An investigation

by the Alberta Ombudsman into the Foster Care Program"
(Edmonton, March 1981), p. 48.

[9]This may change. In September 1982 the newly elected
government announced its intention to phase out the Department
of Northern Saskatchewan.

[10]Correspondence from N. Duane Adams, Deputy Minister,
Saskatchewan Social Services, 8 January 1982.

[11]Ibid.

[12]H. Philip Hepworth, *Foster Care and Adoption in Canada* (Ottawa:
Canadian Council on Social Development, 1980), p. 119.

[13]Manitoba, Child Welfare Directorate, The Manitoba Indian
Adoption Program" (Information given to the sixth meeting of the
National Commission Inquiry on Indian Health, March 1980), p. 2.

[14]Background information prepared for Kimelman Review
Committee on Indian and Métis Adoptions and Placements.

[15]Correspondence to the author, 4 August 1981.

[16]Correspondence from R. A. Quigg,New Brunswick, Department
of Social Services, 10 November 1981.

[17]Adoption statistics provided by Canada Department of Indian
Affairs, Social Development Directorate, Headquarters.

[18]Correspondence from F. J. Simms, Director of Child Welfare,
Newfoundland and Labrador Department of Social Services, 19
March 1982.

[19]Correspondence from Ross N. Findlater, Director of Child
Welfare, Yukon Territory, 7 September 1982.

[20]Statistics Canada, Demography Division.

[21]Canada, Department of Health and Welfare, *Canada Assistance
Plan — Annual Report 1979-1980* (Ottawa, 1980), p.13.

[22]Chris Bagley, "Total Child Welfare for the Eighties" (Paper
prepared for the Canadian Child in the Eighties Conference,
Mount Saint Vincent Univerity, March 1981), p. 35.

[23]Alberta, Office of the Ombudsman, "An Investigation" p. 48.

[24]This excerpt was taken from the draft of a memorandum to
Cabinet, Dated July 1981.

[25]Garry (not his real name) related his experience during a
discussion whith the author, May 1982.

[26]Renate Andres, "The Apprehension of Native Children,"*Ontario
Indian"*, vol. 4, no. 5 (April 1981), p. 35; and Mary Charlotte
McMullen, "Preserving the Indian Family," *Children's Legal
Rights Journal,* vol. 2, no. 6 (May/June)1981, pp. 33-34.

[27]In conversation with the author, September 1981.

[28]*Globe and Mail,* 14 April 1982.

[29]Indian Homemakers' Association of British Columbia "The Family Unit Concert" (Vancouver 1981), p. 1.

[30]British Columbia Native Women's Society, "Proposal for Recommended Legislative Enactment with Respect to Rights for Native Indian Children and Protection of Native Indian Children by Independent Indian Bands" (Proposal presented at the society's annual conference, Kamloops, 1979.

CHAPTER 3:

IDENTIFYING THE PROBLEM AND ITS CAUSES

It is now conceded by almost everyone in the field that the child welfare system has not operated in the best interest of Native children, families and communities. The evidence contained in the statistics presented in the previous chapter is overwhelming. In fact, a 1980 meeting of child welfare experts from across Canada referred to the plight of Native children as a "national tragedy."[1]

While most people in the child welfare field may agree there is a problem, there is not universal agreement on the exact nature or extent of it. This is to be expected. The problem in regard to child welfare services for Native Peoples is multi-faceted. One particular aspect of it may be of great significance and concern to those living in one province, but of little or no interest to people in a neighbouring province.

Nor is there likely to be a national consensus on the causes of the problem. Once again, this is entirely reasonable and to be expected Unfortunately, there is no single, simple cause of the problem amenable to a single, simple solution. A multitude of factors contribute to the disproportionately large number of Native children who enter and remain in the care of child welfare authorities.

The balance of this chapter will discuss those causal factors that appear to be of primary significance on a national basis. The issue of jurisdiction will be outlined, as will the difficulties generated by a clash of two distinct cultures. In addition, the implications of the economic position of Native Peoples, the misuse of alcohol, and the practice of placing children in residential schools will be discussed as factors that may contribute to the problem.

CONTRIBUTING FACTORS

Jurisdictional Disputes

If there is one factor that has fuelled the problem more than any other, it is the continual dispute between the federal and some provincial governments over which has the legal mandate to provide child welfare services on reserves. This issue, which has already been discussed to some extent in chapter 1, is perhaps the greatest impediment to achieving a long-term solution.

The federal-provincial battle has resulted in a vast disparity in the quality and quantity of child welfare services available to status Indians in different parts of the country. Generally speaking, services to Indians still vary from being "unsatisfactory to appalling," as Hawthorn concluded in 1966.[2]

The jurisdictional factor has been of particular importance in three provinces: Alberta, Saskatchewan and Manitoba. None of those provinces has ever had a province-wide agreement with the federal government, formal or informal, to extend its child welfare services to reserves.[3] It was the case in those provinces for the most part, that many families living on-reserve who experienced difficulties received little if any support or assistance from provincial child welfare officials. Only when a child's life was, quite literally, considered to be in danger would the province step in. The assistance provided at that point was almost inevitably the apprehension of the child. In such cases, no preventive or preparatory assistance had been provided the family prior to apprehension. Nor was follow-up work done with the family afterwards, again because the provinces did not consider it to be within their jurisdiction.

The implications of this position should be fairly obvious. A child who has to be apprehended because his life is in danger, is likely to have suffered servere psychological or emotional damage. If there is no assistance given the family after a child's apprehension, the probability of the child being able to return home is remote. In addition, the chances of the child being placed in successful adoption or foster homes are also reduced because of the potential for emotional disturbance as a result of his experience. This probably explains why Native children are less likely to be placed for adoption than non-Indian children. They become "stuck" in the system.

Fortunately, by the late 1970s and early 1980s, the position of some of the three provinces appeared to be moderating. It is clear, however, that prior to this moderation some Indian children were, and probably still are, suffering as a result of this particular federal-provincial argument. A few may even have died. If the benefits of child welfare programs are provided only in a "life and death' situation, the death of some children, by definition, is almost inevitable.

The effects of the jurisdictional dispute are well known to federal officials. In the draft of a memorandum prepared for Cabinet to secure federal approval for a child welfare agreement with the province and Indian bands in Manitoba, the jurisdictional and financial dispute was recognized, as were the effects:

Experience has revealed social factors which must be considered in designing and administering child welfare services to Indian people. Several of these factors have been catalogued in the the following ...
— Indian people residing on reserves do not have access to statutory child welfare and preventive social services comparable to other citizens.
— the several basic arrangements to meet the needs of Indian children and families lack a significant preventive thrust, that is they do not strive to meet the needs of children in their parental homes and do not support wholesome family life.
— services to children and families in Indian communities have been grossly inadequate by any recognized standard.[4]

As the draft memorandum also pointed out, Canada is a signatory to the United Nations Declaration of the Rights of the Child. One of the fundamental principles enshrined in that document is that children have a right to be protected against all forms of cruelty and neglect. In Canada, however, the protection afforded by the state has been denied to some children and families for no other reason than that they are Indian.

The jurisdictional dispute resulted in a situation that was discriminatory and a clear violation of the UN Rights of the Child. It has both contributed to and perpetuated the highly disproportionate number of Native children who entered and remained in the care of child welfare authorities. Unfortunately, although there has been some improvement, it is impossible to state that this particular form of discrimination is not still occurring in some parts of Canada in 1982.

Cultural Conflicts

The jurisdictional battle is not the only issue that must be confronted if the flaws in child welfare that adversely affect Native people are to be rectified. Even in those jurisdictions where child welfare services are available to Native families, the number of Native children in care is still highly disproportionate. The major contributing factor in this instance is a service delivery system that is not always culturally appropriate or compatible with Native customs, values and traditions.

The design, development and delivery of child welfare services in Canada is the responsibility of child care workers, social workers, lawyers and judges, of whom very few are Native. Only a handful will have taken courses in Native studies during their professional education. Most people who work in the child welfare field, in other words, have little understanding of the profound differences in child-rearing practices and beliefs that distinguish Native from non-Native people.

Historically, both Indian and Inuit people exhibited a real fondness for children.[5] In fact, the evidence suggests that Native people treated their children with more kindness and gentleness than did European parents. Furthermore, Native children occupied a more privileged position in society than did their European counterparts. [6] As a result, the use of corporal or physical punishment was virtually unknown. [7] In fact, the Inuit considered it demeaning for an adult to become angered with or annoyed by a child.[8]

A pacifistic approach to child rearing meant that Native families adopted other means of socializing and disciplining their children. It was believed that children learned by imitation, so the concept of the adult-as-role-model was fundamentally important. The development of positive and appropriate behaviour in children was fostered by public opinion and the use of community approval or disapproval. Humour and teasing were employed as a means of discipline in both Indian and Inuit society.[9]

This unique approach to raising children meant that, generally speaking, Native children had a much greater degree of independence and autonomy. Parents whom Europeans would call "permissive" were the norm in Native society. An Indian elder summarized this distinct view of child rearing when he spoke of

> the customs that forbid making a child do what he does not want to do. The norm for acting or not acting is "I want to" or "I don't want to" not the rightness or wrongness of the deed.

Feeling, not logical reasoning, is what determines performance.[10]

Native people also had a distinct and different concept of the family. Unlike the nuclear family definition most commonly used by non-Native people, the term "family" had a much broader meaning for Native people and included grandparents, aunts, uncles and cousins. The family for Native people was what most people refer to as the "extended family."

Implicit in the Native notion of family was a belief that the responsibility for raising children rests with all the members of a family, not only with a child's parents. Grandparents, in particular, have traditionally played a very important role in child rearing. [11] Even more distinct from Euro-Canadian tradition was the belief that the community as a whole had a legitimate role and, indeed, a responsibility to participate in the rearing and caring of all children.[12]

There are many other examples of distinctive approaches to child rearing that were shared by many Native people. For example, there were children who were born out of wedlock but the concept of illegitimacy was virtually unknown. As one Indian elder explained, in many tribes the mother of an "illegitimate" child had the right to name the father. Even if the male denied it, the mother's word was accepted by the tribe, so that the child had a father. From that point on, the man's family took responsibility for the child, who was accorded the same honour and status as if he or she were the "legitimate" child.[13]

Other cultural differences had a less direct but still substantial effect on how Native children were raised. Native people were much less materialistic than Euro-Canadians and more people-oriented.[14] And, control of emotions was a cultural norm and explains why Native people were often referred to as stoics.[15]

Many of the traditional Indian and Inuit child-rearing practices and beliefs discussed above still exist to a remarkable degree in the Native community. The Big Grassy Band in northwestern Ontario is a perfect example.

The Big Grassy Reserve, located near Rainy River, has approximately 200 residents. When people leave the reserve, they often move to Winnipeg, which is the nearest large urban centre. In 1981, the Winnipeg Children's Aid Society filed an application in the Manitoba courts for guardianship of a child whose mother was a registered member of the Big Grassy Band. The band attempted to block the CAS application and filed their own application for guardianship. The case hinged on the band's argument that they should be considered a person within the meaning of Manitoba's Child Welfare Act.[16] The court eventually ruled against the band.

Arguing that an Indian band is a person may seem strange to most non-Native people. It is a concept most would find difficult to understand. In fact, it reflects a belief in the notion of the community as family. It is based on a fundamentally different view of the individual's role in and relationship to society. It is also an example of a culturally based belief about children and families shared by many Native people that is markedly different from those of the dominant culture.

Native people have a long tradition of interdependence — or what we would now label as "self-help." Native society was constituted of relatively small political units or communities that had to be self-sufficient. Because they were small, the welfare of the community was heavily dependent on the welfare of each individual member of that community. The welfare of each child, therefore, was a matter of legitimate concern not only to his parents, but to the community as a whole. The importance of mutual help and self-reliance was heightened after contact with Europeans. The customs, values and traditions of Native people were overwhelmed and severely threatened by those of the Europeans who emigrated to North America in massive numbers. The survival of a distinct and unique culture was at stake.

Survival as a group is still of paramount importance to Native people. As Gerald Wilkinson, the director of the National Indian Youth Council in the United States put it, "Their goals are not simply to survive, but to survive as a community, not just to survive as an individual but to survive as a group."[17] Civil rights takes on a very different meaning as a result. The individual rights of Native people are of lesser importance and at times may have to be subjugated to collective rights if the survival of the collectivity is threatened.

The importance accorded group or collective rights is yet another factor that distinguishes Native and non-Native values. It influences the relationship between families and communities, which Native people believe is appropriate and legitimate. In particular, Native people believe that the community has not only the right but a reponsibility to become involved in Native family life. As Wilkinson said:

The American Indian people are a family. Family is really what a tribe is all about.... The Indian family is in a lot of trouble, and that means that Indian people as a whole are in a lot of trouble because a tribe simply cannot withstand the disintegration of its families. The family is the tribe, and it is this kind of relationship that keeps people going.[18]

The Royal Commission on Family and Children's Law in British Columbia also encountered the issue of individual rights versus band rights. The commission, chaired by the Honourable Mr. Justice Thomas Berger of the British Columbia Supreme Court, considered the conflict between provincial adoption policies and Indian values and customs. It was commonly accepted by provincial authorities that an Indian mother had a right to request that her child be placed in a non-Native home. Her wishes would normally be respected because existing adoption practice affirms the right of individual choice. As the commission discovered, however, this practice fails to acknowledge the existence and legitimacy of band rights. "The majority of Indian people with whom we have discussed this matter believe that the Band should always be notified of the birth of a child to any of its members; that the rights of the Band supersede those of the individual."[19]

The example cited above suggests that Native people have a distinct and unique value system manifest in customs and traditions that have been passed down from generation to generation. Their particular approach to child rearing may still prevail in Native communities. In other words, there may still be child-rearing norms and standards that differentiate Native and non-Native people.

Therein lies the potential for difficulty. A system of child welfare is based on certain beliefs held by members of the dominant culture. Those beliefs evolve into normative standards of child rearing and define which practices should be considered good or bad, proper or improper. A problem arises if one set of standards is applied to a group with a different set of norms. Several observers have suggested that this is precisely what has happened to Native people, not only in Canada but in other countries as well, as they come into contact with child welfare services. A different approach to child rearing may have resulted in Native people receiving inappropriate and, perhaps, even discriminatory treatment by the child welfare system.

Part of the problem may rest with the legislation, regulations and policies that describe the purpose and nature of a child welfare system. Adoption policy, as the Canadian Council on Children and Youth points out, is one example of how the system has the potential to discriminate against Native people.[20]

Historically, it was common in Inuit and Indian societies for a child who was orphaned or abandoned to be taken in and raised by a relative

71

— a practice called custom adoption. In some instances, a child might even be "given" to his or her grandparents, if they no longer had children at home in order to prevent them from becoming lonely. Children were so valued that adults who had no children were considered to be disadvantaged, to use a modern term.

The Northwest Territories and Quebec are the only jurisdictions that officially recognize and sanction custom adoptions. Not only does the practice still exist, it is so common that of the 82 adoption placements made by the N.W.T. Department of Social Services in 1981, 42 or 51.5 percent, were custom adoptions.[21]

In most if not all other jurisdictions in Canada, custom adoptions would probably not be recognized as legal adoptions. By and large, existing adoption policy is based on the premise that an adopted child should not know his or her natural parents. This severing of familial ties is not an element of custom adoption practice, nor is it considered desirable. A long-standing tradition of Native Peoples is ignored, in other words, and this may explain why a majority of Native children have had to be placed for adoption in non-Native homes.

The Berger royal commission also considered the issue of custom adoption. The report presented an excellent summary of the argument being made here:

> Furthermore, we note that the current concept of adoption, in white society, is a relatively new concept. In fact, adoption is as old as man. It has been practised in many different cultures in many different ways. The North American white concept of adoption as a function of child welfare — involving the placing of children with strangers and the complete severing of natural parental ties, including the possibility of inheritance, is a relatively recent development in adoption and seems to reflect the realities of a highly mobile, nuclear-family-oriented, urban, industrial society. To impose this style of adoption on our native Indian population and to call their custom adoptions something less — i.e. guardianship — would be, in our opinion, inappropriate.[22]

Shortcomings that may exist in child welfare legislation and policies are not unexpected. After all, they have been drafted by legislators, lawyers and policy analysts, few of whom have been Native people. Even the language in which they are written may itself be value-laden and culture-specific. As one observer suggested about Saskatchewan's Family Services Act: "It is useful to recognize that the Act contains many words that must be understood to have a special cultural meaning that is not intelligible to people of all cultures."[23]

An additional problem may result not from what the statutes or policies say necessarily, but from what they are interpreted to mean. The wording of child welfare legislation is often very general and even vague. Statutes define children in need of protection as those who are "without adequate care or supervision"[24] or "without proper or competent supervision,"[25] for example. They stipulate the grounds on which children can be apprehended and removed from families. Such grounds include children "living in circumstances that are unfit or improper."[26]

But what constitutes "adequate care" or "proper supervision"? And what, precisely, is meant by "unfit circumstances"? These are extremely broad, value-laden concepts. They do not pertain to absolute conditions and must be defined and interpreted by judges, lawyers and social workers, who, as we have said, are rarely Native people.

The question, of course, is whether those who must give meaning to child welfare legislation can do so while still accommodating differences that are a function of Native culture. An American lawyer believes that in the United States this has not happened. She claims that "most state social workers and judges who determine whether a child is 'neglected' or not, were unaware of Indian cultural differences and what they viewed as neglect often was an alternative, yet acceptable, lifestyle."[27]

There is also the potential for misunderstanding and discrimination on the part of social workers and child care workers who actually provide child welfare services and who have direct contact with families. If those workers are not Native or have little knowledge of Native values and customs, they may not recognize approaches to child rearing that are acceptable in Native society. One such example can be found in the attitude of Native Peoples to material goods, which an American sociologist has suggested is

> the key to understanding Indian child rearing. It is person oriented. The nature of this upbringing is such as to place great value on relationships with other people in the local community and to place negligible value on objects. The child learns to define himself in a relationship with other people, and not in relationship to such abstractions as "career," or "occupation," or money. While reformers stress objects Indians stress personal relationships.[28]

An additional example of the potential for misunderstanding is the learn-by-imitation approach to raising Native children, invariably and incorrectly labelled as permissive. As Wax suggests, it is ironic that many people who characterize Indian parents as permissive also comment on how well mannered and shy Indian children are, a behaviour not usually considered the result of a permissive upbringing.[29] The greater danger, however, is that this approach to child rearing may be mistakenly interpreted as neglect.[30]

There is also a very real problem in that Native people may misunderstand the ways of the non-Native person. The notion of a child welfare system itself is difficult for many Native people to comprehend. As an Indian elder described it, "Indian people have a very difficult time conforming to the system and to institutions that prevail in this country because they are creatures of individual freedom. It goes against their nature to conform to abstract systems and to formalized rules and regulations that have no objective reality to them."[31] Some observers believe that such misunderstanding can and has resulted in Indian parents voluntarily agreeing to relinquish custody of their children on a temporary basis without fully understanding the implications. The temporary committal of children too often becomes permanent.[32]

It is very difficult to prove categorically that the cultural biases of non-Native people involved in the child welfare system have directly resulted in Native children being taken into care. There have been few, if any, studies on this subject. The observations and examples cited here, however, suggest that this factor may have contributed to some extent to the highly disproportionate number of Native children now in care in Canada. It may very well be that some Native families have been judged by child welfare officials and found "wanting," not because their approaches to child rearing were innately bad or damaging, but simply because they were different. The influence of cultural norms and standards on the placement of Native children in care is a complex issue, but an extremely important one that warrants much more study.

Economic Conditions

Any attempt to explain why such a disproportionately large number of Native children are in care must recognize an additional factor that affects non-Native as well as Native people. To some extent, involvement with the child welfare system may be a function of poverty.

The National Council of Welfare is a citizens group that advises the federal minister of health and welfare on matters pertaining to welfare. The council publishes periodic reports on a variety of issues directly affecting low-income Canadians. In 1979 the council directed its attention to child welfare in Canada. In its report, it concluded that "one fundamental characteristic of the child welfare system ... has not changed appreciably over the years: its clients are still overwhelmingly drawn from the ranks of Canada's poor."[33] The council's report suggested two reasons for this phenomenon. First, poverty induces additional stress and pressure and compounds the already difficult task of raising children. Low-income parents, in other words, are susceptible to additional difficulties that may reduce their ability to properly care for their children. Second, low-income parents are more apt to use public child welfare services than are affluent parents, who can afford the help of psychiatrists, psychologists and social workers in private practice.

If there is one economically disadvantaged group in Canada, it is Native people.[34] Using the National Council of Welfare's argument, it follows that Native parents may experience greater burdens while raising their children than do non-Native parents. This, in turn, may explain why there are more Native children in the care of child welfare authorities. There is a danger, however, in relying too heavily on this argument. The problem is not with the argument itself, but rather with the way it may be interpreted. Some people may twist the argument and draw the inference that poverty inevitably results in poor parenting. In fact, it may be used inappropriately by some to advance the notion that poor people make poor parents.

The fact that the majority of people who use child welfare services are poor is disturbing. In some ways, it may reflect the extent to which society equates money with love, and materialism with the ability to raise children. People in the child welfare field may themselves be guilty. Standards for foster parents, for example, have become increasingly stringent in recent years. But the standards established often refer to tangible, material conditions, such as the number and size of bedrooms and bathrooms. By inference, if you cannot afford to provide the requisite number of bathrooms, you are not as capable and competent a parent.

The setting of standards of care is an important objective for those in the child welfare field. We must ensure, however, that the definition of standards is not restricted exclusively, or even primarily, to material standards. More important are the qualities of love, warmth, compassion, consistency and commitment to children.

Unfortunately, material standards may have played a significant role in the past in determining whether Native parents were fit to look after their children. It is not unreasonable to suggest that some Native children may have come into care primarily because their parents were poor or perceived to be poor, and, therefore, judged to be inadequate as parents. As Sanders stated:

> Provincial child welfare officials have certain cultural values about adequate material standards for home life and about how children should be raised. The differences between the material standards of whites and Indians and the differences between the child rearing attitudes of the two groups has resulted in the excessive apprehension of Indian children.[35]

Once again we see the consequences of a conflict of culture and values. What people in child welfare consider to be "adequate standards" may not be appropriate standards by which to judge Native families. Native people appear to be much less materialistic than other Canadians; they are raised to be people-oriented rather than object-oriented.[36] As a result, they don't necessarily evaluate the success or status of others on the basis of material possessions or the lack of them.

As the National Council of Welfare suggests, there is a correlation between poverty and child welfare. Poverty does impose an additional stress that may result in a greater number of poor children coming into care. But there is another side to the coin. We must recognize that some children may have been taken into care not because they were unloved or unwanted or neglected, but because they were poor. This may be another explanation for the number of Native children in care.

Other Factors

There are many other factors that may contribute to the disproportionate involvement of Native Peoples in the child welfare system. Two are worth noting, in particular, because they are mentioned frequently by Native people—alcohol abuse and placement of children in residential schools.

Alcohol is often cited as one of the reasons there are so many Native children in care, because of the extensive use and abuse of alcohol by many Native people. Alcoholism results in child neglect, which results in the apprehension of children. The Indian Homemakers' Association of British Columbia believes that it is a major factor:

Our own experiences have shown the majority of Indian child apprehensions have been primarily the result of alcohol abuse and cultural clash of white, middle-class standards by social workers.[37]

There is no question that many Native people have a serious problem regulating their alcohol intake, as do many many non-Native people. They must also contend with the stereotype of "the drunk Indian," however, which may adversely influence the decisions of child welfare workers.

Social workers may be more likely to find alcohol abuse in Native families because they are more likely to look for it. And they may use that as an excuse to apprehend more frequently in Native than non-Native families. There have been studies in the United States, for example, that suggest that where the rate of problem drinking among Native and non-Native people was similar, parental neglect was rarely applied to the non-Native person to justify the apprehension of children.[38]

Rather than viewing alcoholism as a cause of child neglect in Native communities, it is more useful to think of it as a symptom of more fundamental and deep-seated problems. It is a consequence of a lack of employment opportunities and of the resulting despair experienced by many Native people. Alcoholism is a symptom of the powerlessness of Native people who are denied the right of self-determination.

Alcoholism in Native communities can be reduced if the problems are rectified. Chris Bagley at the University of Calgary points to a band in Alberta as an example. When employment opportunities increased as a result of oil revenues, the band experienced a concomitant decrease in alcoholism.[39] The problems of neglect in Native families that may result from alcohol abuse will only be resolved, in other words, if the causes of alcoholism are minimized.

Another factor possibly contributing to the problem and often mentioned by Native people results from a policy that is gradually being phased out. Status Indians are especially hostile and bitter about the practice of placing Indian children in residential schools. Until the late 1950s, many Indian children were removed at an early age and sent to live in residential schools. The schools were usually a long distance from the reserves, so that most Indian children would return to their parents only during the summer. Residential schools were a traumatic and depersonalizing experience for many children. As mentioned previously, it was common practice for children to be punished for speaking their own language instead of English. One former student recalled that the nuns who ran the school he attended referred to the children by their band numbers rather than by name.[40] Fortunately, the damage being done to Indian children, families and communities was finally recognized, and most residential schools have been closed. But the effects are still felt. Children placed in residential schools lost meaningful contact with their families and communities. There was discontinuity and disruption in the centuries-old process of passing down from generation to generation customs and traditions about a multitude of issues, including methods of child rearing. Some Native children may be coming into care essentially because their parents did not learn how to raise children in the traditional way as a result of their own placement in residential schools. As the Indian Homemakers' Association of British Columbia argues:

> The effects of residential schools on this generation of parents must be taken into serious consideration since the Indian parents of today were the generation of residential school children yesterday.[42]

CONCLUSIONS

The placement of Indian children in residential schools, alcohol abuse, the disadvantaged economic situation experienced by many Native people, cultural misunderstanding, and the jurisdictional stand-off may all combine to explain, at least in part, why so many Native children are in care. Even these explanations may be of secondary importance, however. They may not be as causal as they are symptomatic of the real problem.

It is often easy to forget that Native Peoples have historically been, and continue to be, the objects of policies of colonialization. Colonialization is the process by which one group extends its control and authority over other peoples or territories to derive certain benefits. Pete Hudson and Brad McKenzie of the University of Manitoba have done an excellent job of linking child welfare to colonialization.[43] They suggest that until the process of colonialization is understood and acknowledged, attempts to improve child welfare services for Native Peoples will be problematic.

There are three attributes, in particular, that describe a colonial relationship. First, the ultimate power and decision-making ability is vested in the dominant group. Second, the practices, customs and traditions of the subordinate group are devalued. Third, an interactive feature of a colonial relationship conditions both the colonizer and the colonized to think and behave in certain ways. Often, the response of the colonized will reinforce the negative image of them held by members of the dominant group.

Hudson and McKenzie argue that all of these attributes describe the relationship between Native Peoples and the child welfare system. The decision making and the power rest almost exclusively with non-Native people. Traditional Native approaches to child rearing have been ignored or misunderstood and, therefore, devalued. And the response of Native Peoples often reinforces old stereotypes; for instance, an Indian woman's alcoholism may be exacerbated when her children are taken away from her.

There have been different institutionalized agents of colonialization in the past that have effected the separation of children and families. The health and educational system are two examples, but Hudson and McKenzie believe the child welfare system is as much at fault. And, more importantly, they suggest that this belief is held by many Native people:

> While the present child welfare system may not acknowledge the overt pursuit of colonial objectives, to many Native people there is a striking similarity in the pattern which resulted in the removal of children by the early settlers, the placement of children in the residential school system in the early 20th century, and the patterns associated with the apprehension of native children by child authorities which continue to this day.[44]

Whether they are more symptom than cause, the myriad of complex, contributing factors discussed in this chapter may explain why relatively little effort has been devoted to attacking the inadequacies of the child welfare system as it affects Native people. The multitude of factors also suggests that no simple solution exists that will be an immediate panacea. There are, however, a variety of constructive measures we can adopt that will eventually reduce the number of Native children in care. Some of these changes will be described in the following chapters.

Notes to Chapter 3

1*Globe and Mail*, 19 June 1980.

2H. B. Hawthorn et al, *A Survey of the Contemporary Indians of Canada*, vol. I (Ottawa: Canada Department of Indian Affairs, 1966), p. 327.

3There was an attempt in 1981-82 to establish a province-wide agreement in Manitoba. The specifics of the agreement are discussed in chapter 6.

4Draft memorandum to Cabinet, July 1981.

5Diamond Jenness, *The Indians of Canada* (Ottawa: Canada Department of Northern Affairs and Natural Resources, 1955), pp. 158, 420.

6Canadian Council on Children and Youth, *Admittance Restricted: The Child as Citizen in Canada* (Ottawa, 1978), p. 124.

7Jenness, *Indians*, pp. 151-52.

8Jean Briggs, *Aspects of Inuit Value Socialization*, Mecury Series, paper no. 56 (Ottawa: National Museums of Canada, 1979), p. 17.

9See Briggs, *Aspects of Inuit;* Renate Andres, "The Apprehension of Native Children," *Ontario Indian*, vol. 4, no. 5 (April 1981), p. 37; Melissa Lazore, *A Perspective on Contemporary Native Peoples* (Ottawa: Canada Department of Indian and Northern Affairs, 1980), p. 8; and Ann Metcalf, "A Model for Treatment in a Native American Family Service Center" (Oakland, Calif.: Urban Indian Child Resource Center, 1978), p. 10.

10Sylvester M. Morey and Olivia L. Gilliam, eds., *Respect for Life: Report of a Conference at Harper's Ferry, West Virginia, on the Traditional Upbringing of American Indian Children* (Garden City, N. Y.: Waldorf Press, 1972), p. 66.

11Ibid., pp. 83-84.

12See Jenness, *Indians*, p. 152; Lazore, *A Perspective,* p. 8; and British Columbia Royal Commission on Family and Children's Law, *Tenth Report of the Royal Commission on Family and Children's Law: Native Families and the Law* (Vancouver, May 1975), p. 22.

13Morey and Gilliam, *Respect for Life*, pp. 98-99.

14Anne LaFontaine, "Where We Came From: A Review of Traditional Indian Family Life" (Ottawa: National Indian Brotherhood, 1979), p. 14.

15Andres, "Apprehension," p. 37.

16Provincial Judge Raymond H. Harris, *In the Matter of the Child Welfare Act R.S.M. 1974 and the Indian Act of Canada*, Provincial

Judges Court (Family Division) of Winnipeg, 24 August 1981, p. 4.
[17]Gerald Thomas Wilkinson, "On Assisting Indian People," *Social Casework*, vol. 61, no. 8 (October 1980), p. 453. See also Jack Sissons, *Judge of the Far North* (Toronto: McClelland and Stewart, 1968).

[18]Wilkinson, "On Assisting," p. 451.

[19]British Columbia Royal Commission on Family and Children's Law, *Tenth Report*, p. 31.

[20]Canadian Council on Children and Youth, *Admittance Restricted*, pp. 133-34.

[21]Correspondence from Diane Doyle, Director of Child Welfare, Northwest Territories, 10 March 1982.

[22]British Columbia Royal Commission on Family and Children's Law, *Tenth Report*, p. 40. For further discussion of custom adoption practices, see Douglas Sanders, *Family Law and Native Peoples: Background Paper* (Ottawa: Law Reform Commission of Canada, 1975), pp. 4, 62-73; and British Columbia Royal Commission on Family and Children's Law, *Fifth Report of the Royal Commission on Family and Children's Law: Part VII — Adoption* (Vancouver, 1975).

[23]Andres, "Apprehension," p. 34.

[24]The Child Welfare Act, *Statutes of Newfoundland* 1972, c. 37 s.2(a.1)(i).

[25]The Family Services Act, *Revised Statutes of Saskatchewan* 1978 c. F-7, s. 15(a).

[26]Ibid., s. 15(b).

[27]Mary Charlotte McMullen, *"Preserving the Indian Family," Children's Legal Rights Journal,* vol. 2, no. 6 (May/June 1981), p. 32.

[28]Murray L. Wax, "Social Structure and Child Rearing Practices of North American Indians" in *Nutrition, Growth and Development of American Indian Children,* eds. William M. Moore et al, DHEW publication no. (NIH) 72-26 (Washington, D.C.: U.S. Government Printing Office, 1972), p. 206.

[29]Ibid., p. 205.

[30]Metcalf, *"Model for Treatment,"* p. 10.

[31]Morey and Gilliam, *Respect for Life*, p. 150; Sanders, *Family Law*, pp. 119-20.

[32]McMullen, *Preserving*, p. 33; British Columbia Royal Commission on Family and Children's Law, *Tenth Report*, p. 16.

[33]National Council of Welfare, *In the Best Interests of the Child* (Ottawa, 1979), p. 2.

[34] For evidence, see Canada, Department of Indian and Northern Affairs, *Indian Conditions: A Survey* (Ottawa, 1980).

[35] Sanders, *Family Law*, p. 118. See also Pete Hudson and Brad McKenzie, "Child Welfare and Native Peoples: The Extension of Colonialism," *Social Worker*, vol. 49, no. 2 (Summer 1981), p. 66.

[36] LaFontaine, "Where We Came From," p. 14.

[37] Indian Homemakers' Association of British Columbia, "The Family Unit Concept" (Vancouver, 1981). p. 3.

[38] McMullen, *Preserving*, p. 33.

[39] Chris Bagley, "Total Child Welfare for the Eighties" (Paper prepared for the Canadian Child in the Eighties Conference, Mount Saint Vincent University, March 1981), pp. 27-28.

[40] Albert Angus, "The Thunderchild," *Queens Journal Magazine*, vol. 3, no.1 (November 1981), p. 2.

[41] The experience of Indians living in the United States was the same. See Barbara Brooks Johnson, "The Indian Child Welfare Act of 1978: Implications for Practice," *Child Welfare*, vol. 60, no. 7 (July/August 1981).

[42] Indian Homemakers' Association of British Columbia, "Family Unit," p. 4. The U.S. experience was similar; see, for example, McMullen, *Preserving*, p. 34.

[43] Hudson and McKenzie, "Child Welfare."

[44] Ibid., p. 66.

CHAPTER 4

FINDING SOLUTIONS:
THE JURISDICTION ISSUE

Matters of public policy are inevitably subject to political considerations. An issue that affects a majority of the population, especially if it is perceived to be a problem, is more likely to receive attention than one affecting a minority.

Generally speaking, it is also true that those responsible for formulating public policy are more likely to address themselves to problems that are easily resolved. After all, they must demonstrate their competence to solve public problems to their political masters, who in turn want evidence of their successes to present to the electorate.

The flaws in the provision of child welfare services to Native children and families cannot compete for the public's attention with issues such as inflation or unemployment. Nor is it a problem for which there are quick answers. In spite of this fact, even those who should know better demand instant solutions and when they aren't forthcoming, turn their attention to other matters.

Permanent solutions are impossible until it is recognized that they cannot be implemented quickly or easily. The difficulties addressed in this volume have not developed overnight, nor will they be resolved immediately. This is not to suggest, however, that the problems are intractable or that there is no hope for constructive change. On the contrary, a variety of specific, concrete steps can be taken that would result in short-term improvements. They are intended primarily to redress the problems caused by cultural misunderstanding and will be described in chapter 5.

A solution to the jurisdictional dispute is also possible, although the complexity of the subject is such that any change is likely to entail a long-term process. Several possible alternatives to resolve the jurisdictional argument will be discussed in this chapter.

OPTIONS FOR CHANGE

The discussion in this chapter will focus exclusively on the most problematic aspect of the jurisdictional battle—that is, which level of government has the legislative mandate and financial responsibility to provide child welfare services to Indian residents of reserves. It is possible to delineate four broad options for resolving this problem. Not surprisingly, there is unlikely to be consensus on the preferred option. The federal government is not likely to choose the option desired by the provinces. In fact, it is not at all certain that provincial governments would agree on an option among themselves. The organizations representing Native people are more likely to favour the same options, but even then unanimity is not certain. The elements of each alternative will be discussed briefly, followed by a description of some of the shortcomings of each.

Option 1: Federal-Provincial Agreements

One method of attacking the jurisdictional problem would require that the federal government enter into formal agreements with each of the provinces to provide child welfare services on reserves. Such agreements already exist in some provinces, but they would have to be extended to the other provinces as well. If this option were to succeed, the level of service provided would have to be expanded beyond the terms of existing agreements. There would also have to be a complete overhaul of arrangements for financial compensation to the provinces.

Shortcomings
Given the current state of federal-provincial relations, the likelihood of the federal and many of the provincial governments entering new agreements is questionable. It must be remembered that these negotiations would primarily involve the western provinces—with which the federal government (as of 1982) has the most acrimonious relations.

There is also no indication that Saskatchewan and Alberta, for example, are any more likely to enter such an agreement in the future than they have been in the past. In addition, most Native organizations and the provincial associations of status Indians, in particular, would likely oppose this option.

Finally, the pursuit of this option would simply skirt the problem of jurisdiction rather than resolve it. Even where formal agreements now exist, there is disagreement as to whether the ultimate responsibility rests with the federal or the provincial governments.

Option 2: Provincial Legislation

The second option would require that the formal legislative and financial responsibility to provide child welfare services on reserves be vested with provincial governments. This could be done by amending provincial child welfare statutes and perhaps even the Indian Act to include an explicit statement about provincial responsibility. It might be accomplished by the implementation of a separate piece of child welfare legislation that would refer exclusively to Native people.

Undoubtedly there are other ways of implementing this option, but its potential for success would probably depend largely on a financial incentive offered by the federal government.

Shortcomings
As was the case with the first option, this option would definitely be opposed by many provincial governments. There is no reason to believe that provinces which have insisted in the past that child welfare on reserves is a federal responsibility are going to change their position.

In addition, of all the options this one would likely be opposed most vehemently by organizations of Native people and especially the status Indian political associations. The involvement of provincial governments on reserves, for any reason, is viewed with suspicion and mistrust. Any expansion of provincial authority is now considered by many Indian people, especially since the 1969 White Paper, as a real threat to their survival. While an expansion and improvement of child welfare services is the goal, it will be rejected outright by many Indian people if it is to be achieved under the authority of the provincial governments.

Option 3: Federal Legislation

Option number three would see the federal government accepting and assuming full responsibility for the provision of child welfare programs on all reserves in Canada. This responsibility could be assumed by amending the Indian Act or by implementing a new piece of federal legislation similar to the United States Indian Child Welfare Act.

If this option were adopted, the federal government could fulfill its responsibilities in several different ways. It might choose to deliver services directly, through local and regional offices and using Indian Affairs employees. It might establish a separate Indian child welfare and family services authority as a new branch of the Department of Indian Affairs. Or it could empower individual bands to develop and deliver their own programs. This particular option is preferred by many Native organizations.[1]

Shortcomings
Although this option would quite likely be supported by most organizations representing status Indians, it is questionable that it would find favour with the federal government. In the first place, it would entail a significant increase in federal expenditures. A system of services would have to be developed in those regions where child welfare services are not now provided to residents of reserves. And the level and quality of existing programs would have to be vastly improved.

The federal government's strongest objection may be more philosophical than financial, however. As discussed in chapter 1, the 1969 White Paper on Indian policy recommended a transfer of direct federal responsibility for Indian people to the provinces. Even though the federal government shelved the White Paper, many people believe that the devolution of authority to the provinces is still the operative philosophy governing Indian Affairs. This speculation has been confirmed somewhat by a senior provincial official.[2] He indicated that during a closed-door meeting with some of his provincial colleagues, the Minister of Indian Affairs bluntly and candidly told them that the transfer of responsibility for Indians to the provinces was still the ultimate goal of his government and that "they had better be ready for it."

The pursuit of this option is contrary to the direction in which Indian Affairs appears to be heading. In 1982, the federal government was planning to commission a study on the feasibility of Indian child welfare legislation. If it undertakes such a study however, it may not be because the government is seriously considering the possibility of federal legislation, but in order to respond to an increasing interest expressed by Indian associations in this type of legislation.

While many provinces would welcome any move by the federal government to assert and exercise authority for child welfare on reserves, there is no guarantee that support would be unanimous. It is entirely possible that some provinces, Quebec in particular, would object to this alternative. The provision of child welfare services by the federal government may be seen as an incursion into provincial jurisdiction, even though Indians are a federal responsibility.

Option 4: Native Sovereignty

If they have thought about it at all, very few non-Native people will accept the notion that Indian, Métis and Inuit Peoples are distinct and sovereign nations. The concept of Native sovereignty is neither new nor totally without foundation, however, and warrants consideration.

Status Indians, in particular, have often challenged the authority of provincial governments in any area that affects them directly. Some are now challenging the federal government's authority, as evidenced by lobbying done by Indian organizations in Britain to block the patriation of the constitution. Some Indian people, of course, have never accepted or recognized the authority of any other government—federal, provincial or band. There are residents of reserves in southern Ontario and Quebec who, as members of the Five Nations Confederacy, are adherents of traditional religious, social and political customs and practices known as the Long House. The Long House operates independently of band councils, which are considered to be a Euro-Canadian model imposed on Indians by the federal government.

The fourth option is philosophically grounded in this notion of sovereignty. This alternative does not require a change in either federal or provincial legislation in as much as it ignores both. It would entail a unilateral declaration of a band's exclusive authority to provide child welfare services to members of the band. It is essentially the option taken by the Spallumcheen Band in British Columbia and it may be the preferred option of other Indians. Delegates at the Ontario Chiefs Conference passed the following resolution on 3 December 1981:

> BE IT RESOLVED that the child welfare agencies of Ontario and Manitoba shall not remove our children from our reserves, and shall return to their bands those of our children whom they have removed in the past;
>
> AND BE IT FURTHER RESOLVED that we the Indian Nations in Ontario shall create our own Indian child welfare laws, policies and programs, based on the protection of children and the preservation of their Indian culture within the Indian family.[3]

Shortcomings
A band's declaration of exclusive responsibility for child welfare is a meaningless statement if the human and financial resources to exercise that authority do not exist. Very few bands are in a position to finance their own program without additional funding. Not surprisingly, neither the federal nor the provincial governments are likely to provide the money unconditionally.

There is an additional much more serious problem with this option. Even if individual bands were able to go it alone, their legal position would be very tenuous. If challenged in court, the unilateral assertion of band authority may be found illegal and invalid.

There is, of course, a possible fifth option which is the maintenance of the status-quo—but it will not be presented as a serious option. The situation described in previous chapters speaks for itself and clearly suggests that maintaining things as they are is neither a desirable nor an acceptable alternative.

Of the four options discussed above, more attention has been given to the third option, which would necessitate new, or amendments to existing, federal legislation. To a large extent, interest in this particular alternative has been heightened by the experience in the United States and, in particular, by the implementation in 1978 of the United States Indian Child Welfare Act.

There are many parallels between the experiences of Native people in both countries with the child welfare system. As a result, a brief discussion of the development and intent of the U.S. act may be useful to those who are considering the feasibility of federal Indian child welfare legislation in Canada.

THE UNITED STATES INDIAN CHILD WELFARE ACT

The Indian Child Welfare Act was signed into law in the United States on 8 November 1978. It was the culmination of a lengthy campaign to lobby Congress to rectify the shortcomings in the U.S. child welfare system that had an adverse effect on Indian families and children.

The act was the Americans' response to a situation remarkably similar to that in Canada. Surveys conducted in the 1960s and 1970s indicated that a highly disproportionate number of Indian children were involved in the child welfare system. If anything, the figures in the U.S. were even worse than the Canadian statistics.[4]

The reasons cited for the large number of American Indian children in care are also similar to those described in the previous chapter.

American law professor Russel Barsh, for example, pointed to the ignorance and bias of non-Indian caseworkers, state licensing standards that reflected middle-class values, and subjective judicial decisions made about children that reflected culturally based values in direct conflict with Indian values.[5]

The intent of the act was to reduce the number of Indian children being removed from their own families and placed in non-Indian homes. In doing so, it was hoped that Indian families would be stabilized and strengthened.

In order to achieve this objective, the legislation authorized the transfer of jurisdiction for the welfare of Indian children from the state and federal governments to Indian tribes. In particular, it formally recognized the authority and jurisdiction of tribal courts in matters pertaining to the custody of American Indian children. The jurisdiction of the tribal courts not only covered children living on reservations, but extended to children living off the reservation who were members of, or eligible for membership in, the tribe.

In regions where such authority had already been formally vested with state governments, the Indian Child Welfare act allowed tribes to apply to reassume their jurisdiction. In addition, the act also gave Indian parents and tribes the right to notice of hearing and right of intervention in any state action involving Indian children.

The U.S. legislation also established minimum standards to govern the removal of Indian children from their own families and to facilitate their placement in homes reflecting Indian culture. The preferred adoption placements for Indian children, for example, were:(1) a member of the child's extended family; (2) other members of the child's tribe; or (3) other Indian families.

The Indian Child Welfare Act was hailed by most people in the U.S. as a significant and positive step towards improving child welfare services provided to Indian families and communities. Certain aspects of the legislation have come in for criticism, however.

Barsh is one of those who argues that the act does not contain enough preventive measures. It concentrates too much on the procedures to be followed after a family has broken up and not enough on steps that could be taken to prevent a break up in the first place. He states that "the Act does little to alter the conditions that Congress held responsible for the unwarranted break up of Indian families."[6]

Still others argue that the act, in effect, violates the rights of children. Ronald Fischler of the University of Arizona cited several sections he believes place the rights of parents and tribes ahead of the rights of children.[7] The attempt to redress past grievances may have been taken too far, with Indian children still being victimized. As Mary Charlotte McMullen of the Georgetown University Law Centre said:

The Act, in an attempt to address the neglected rights of Indian parents, has taken a 360 degree turn and seems to rely on the belief that Indian parents are never neglectful and that all findings of neglect are based on cutural bias.[8]

Yet another criticism relates more to the implementation of the act than to the statute itself. Many were initially concerned that the act would be jeopardized because of a lack of funds for the services and programs precribed by the legislation.[9] Nancy Tuthill of the American Indian Law Centre recently told a group of Canadian Indian lawyers that those fears have been realized since President Reagan's budget-cutting measures.[10]

The U.S. legislation, not surprisingly, has generated a great deal of interest in Canada. As mentioned, in early 1982 a study of the feasibility of federal Indian child welfare legislation was considered. It should be remembered, though, that the U.S. act itself is of only limited value to Canada. It relies heavily on tribal courts, a system that does not exist in Canada. Furthermore it is grounded in a variety of historical and legal precedents that have treated Indian tribes in the U.S. as quasi-sovereign nations. By contrast, Canada has never formally or legally acknowledged the sovereignty of Indian tribes.[11]

Nevertheless, the U.S. experience with federal child welfare legislation is of significance to Canada both symbolically and practically. The act is a concrete example of the Americans' efforts to deal with a problem that is just as real in Canada. Its very existence increases the demands made on the Canadian government to find solutions. The legislation also involves a realignment of jurisdictional boundaries between the federal and state governments and tribes.[12] The issue of jurisdiction is of even greater importance in the Canadian context. The American experience will be instructive and beneficial for those considering similar legislation in Canada.

There is an additional important aspect to the jurisdictional question that has not yet been mentioned only because it compounds an already complex problem. Assuming there is a resolution of the issue of jurisdiction for child welfare on reserves, what happens when families leave the reserve? The answer will depend primarily on which of the above alternatives are pursued. If the authority for child welfare for Indian people both off- and on-reserve rests with the same body, there is little difficulty. If two different authorities are involved, however, there may be a problem. Quite clearly, the question of jurisdiction for Indian residents who leave the reserve must also be entertained during a discussion of any or all of the options discussed above. Some of the problems pertaining to status Indians living off-reserve may be minimized by several suggestions presented in the next chapter.

Notes to Chapter 4

[1]See, for example, British Columbia Native Women's Society, "Proposal for Recommended Legislative Enactment with Respect to Rights for Native Indian Children and Protection of Native Indian Children by Independent Indian Bands" (Proposal presented at the society's annual conference, Kamloops, 1979), p. 10.

[2]In conversation with the author, September 1981.

[3]Correspondence from Janice Bourdeau, Union of Ontario Indians, 5 January 1982.

[4]See, for example, Steven Unger, ed., *The Destruction of American Indian Families* (New York: Association of American Indian Affairs, 1977).

[5]Russel Lawrence Barsh, "The Indian Child Welfare Act of 1978: A Critical Analysis," *Hastings Law Journal*, vol. 31, (July 1980), pp. 1287-1336.

[6]Ibid., p. 1334.

[7]Ronald S. Fischler, "Protecting American Indian Children," *Social Work*, vol. 25, no. 5 (September), pp. 341-49.

[8]Mary Charlotte McMullen, "Preserving the Indian Family," *Children's Legal Rights Journal*, vol. 2, no. 6 (May/June 1981), p. 36.

[9]Barsh, "Indian Child," pp. 1333-34; and Garry Wamser, "Child Welfare under the Indian Child Welfare Act of 1978: A New Mexico Focus," *New Mexico Law Review*, vol. 10 (Summer 1980), p. 429.

[10]*Leader Post* (Regina), 19 March 1981.

[11]J. Anthony Long, Leroy Little Bear and Menno Boldt, "Federal Indian Policy and Indian Self-Government in Canada: An Analysis of a Current Proposal," *Canadian Public Policy*, vol. 8, no. 2 (Spring 1982), p. 193.

[12]For an excellent discussion of some of the jurisdictional questions being considered in the U.S., see Barbara Brooks Johnson, "American Indian Jurisdiction as a Policy Issue," *Social Work*, vol. 27, no.1 (January 1982), pp. 31-37.

CHAPTER 5

FINDING SOLUTIONS:
THE CLASH OF CULTURES

Many of the problems described in previous chapters may result from a misunderstanding of and failure to accommodate the values, beliefs and customs that distinguish Native Peoples from all other Canadians. Concrete measures to rectify these shortcomings must be taken in conjunction with efforts to resolve the jurisdictional dispute. In fact, these kinds of measures can be implemented more readily.

A variety of constructive changes that can and should be made will be described below. Many will not seem new. Often, they are good, sound recommendations that have been made before but need repeating because they have never been implemented. In some cases, they have been implemented in some jurisdictions and merit the consideration of other provinces and territories. And, finally, some are still evolving as possibilities, but they appear to be realistic and to warrant more serious discussion. Collectively, they may result in a vast improvement in the provision of child welfare services for all Native Peoples, whether living on a reserve, in a rural or remote area, or in a large urban centre.

The proposals discussed in this chapter must be qualified, however. While factors such as alcohol abuse and poverty and the economic status of Native Peoples contribute to the large number of Native children in care, it is beyond the scope of this work to propose changes which might mitigate those problems. The recommendations presented here will pertain only to the child welfare system and will entail changes in existing legislation and in policies, as well as practice. These changes are not mutually exclusive. Nor must they be implemented on a nationwide basis in order to be effective. The nature of the problem is such that changes considered desirable and appropriate for Native Peoples in one region of the country may very well differ from those sought by people in another area. This does not make the resolution of the problems any easier, but is a fact which must be recognized.

There is, however, one inviolate principle the acceptance of which is a prerequisite for improvement. Native people must become more directly involved in and responsible for the design, development and delivery of child welfare services provided to Native families. Only then will the decisions made about Native children be consistent with Native values, customs, traditions and community standards.

There may not always be agreement on when and how to increase the formal responsibility of Native people for child welfare. Exclusive control is the ultimate objective of many and some Native people have already reached that stage —see next chapter. Other Native groups neither want nor are capable of control at this point, however.[1] Native people are scattered along a continuum, ranging from little or no involvement in child welfare at one end to exclusive control at the other end. Until the principle of Native involvement and responsibility for child welfare is broadly accepted, there is little likelihood of any significant change.

The following suggestions apply primarily to provincial and territorial child welfare systems. They have been grouped into two fairly broad categories. The first includes changes that will, or are likely to, entail revisions to existing child welfare legislation and ministerial or province wide policies. The second group involves changes in practice, most of which can probably be developed and followed through at a community level. They might require some procedural changes at a local agency or regional office level, but wouldn't necessarily require amendments to legislation or departmental policy.

LEGISLATIVE AND POLICY CHANGES

A number of specific steps can be taken to strengthen the Native child's link with his culture and to ensure the involvement of Native people in planning for the Native child who is taken into care. A few provinces have already shown the way. British Columbia, for example, recently amended its major child welfare statute and included one of the recommendations of the Berger Royal Commission. The act now requires that notice of hearing

> shall be in writing and served, at least seven clear days before the hearing ... if the Superintendent believes the child is registered, or is entitled to be registered as an Indian under the Indian Act (Canada), to the Band manager or Band social development officer of the Indian Band to which the child belongs.[2]

Bands in British Columbia are now able to keep track of their children, which can facilitate their involvement in planning for that child's future. This change should also help social workers, especially in urban areas, to identify potential placement resources either on-reserve or with a member of the child's extended family.

Nova Scotia goes even further and has a policy that precludes the indiscriminate placement of Indian children in non-Indian homes. It was explained this way:

Because of the understanding of the importance of cultural heritage to the Indian child in his developmental years, approval for the adoption of the Indian child with non-Indian parents will not be given unless it can be demonstrated that such a placement is in the child's best interests.[3]

As a further check, a proposed placement of an Indian child in a non-Indian home must be submitted to a reserve's child welfare committee for approval. The Nova Scotia policy implies that, all things being equal, the best placement for an Indian child is in an Indian home, and appears to place the onus on child welfare workers to prove otherwise.

The importance accorded a Native child's cultural heritage is not as evident in other provinces. Newfoundland and Labrador, however, is one exception. That province's Child Welfare Act was recently amended and now reads:

In determining the best interest of the child for the purpose of this Act the following shall be considered....
(g) the child's cultural and religious heritage....[4]

One area in need of change but which has received relatively little attention, however, is adoption policy. In theory, a registered Indian child does not lose his or her status even if adopted by a non-Indian family. A University of British Columbia law professor, Douglas Sanders, discovered that there is a discrepancy between the theory and reality.[5] Sanders pointed out that there is no statutory requirement that provincial child welfare authorities inform adoptive parents that a child has Indian status. Nor is there a requirement that child welfare officials inform the registrar of status Indians in Ottawa of the adoption of an Indian child. In fact, existing rules of confidentiality make it difficult, if not technicallly illegal in some instances, for provincial authorities to transmit this kind of information. The extent to which child welfare authorities provide such information to adoptive parents and/or the Indian Affairs registrar varies from province to province. Some children may be status Indian and not know it. As Sanders said:

> If the child is never informed that he or she has a claim to Indian status and does not on his or her own inquire of the Registrar, the technical retention of Indian status, the presence of the names on the files in Ottawa, is quite meaningless.[6]

The unique rights of status Indians—including a share of trust funds accruing to bands, access to services such as education that are provided by the federal government, or property rights—may effectively be denied to some status Indian children because of existing provincial adoption legislation and policy.

Justice Berger's royal commission concurred with Sanders and proposed three recommendations designed to overcome this problem. Although directed at the British Columbia government, they can be implemented in other jurisdictions. The commission's report included these suggestions:

> 20. The Superintendent of Child Welfare should be required to convey to the Registrar in the Department of Indian Affairs all relevant information about the adoption of a status Indian child.
> 21. The Superintendent of Child Welfare should be required to notify the adopting parents of the fact that the child is a status Indian, and of his band membership.
> 22. The Superintendent of Child Welfare should be required to notify the child at age 21 of the fact that he or she is a status Indian.[7]

The Yukon Territory is one jurisdiction that has implemented a procedure designed to ensure that status Indian children placed for adoption will receive any benefits rightfully due them. The territorial government automatically informs the Council of Yukon Indians every time an Indian child is placed for adoption. This measure is especially intended to guarantee that such children are registered as eligible beneficiaries of any future land-claim settlement.[8]

There are a variety of other measures that while they may not prevent the removal of a Native child from his own parents, at least increase the possibility of culturally appropriate placements with members of the extended family or other Native people.

The extraordinarily high rate of adoption of status Indian children by non-Indian parents has long been a source of concern. Each time the issue is discussed, there follows a plea to "find" more Indian parents who would like to adopt. The problem, of course, is that the economic position of many is such that they simply do not have the resources to feed an extra mouth. The Berger commission recommended that in cases like this, specialized adoption subsidies should be provided.[9] In other words, Indian families who wanted to adopt Indian children would not be denied for financial reasons alone.

There may also be other factors that impede the adoption of Indian children by Indian people. A social worker employed by the Bella Bella Band in British Columbia recently indicated that there were several families on the reserve who expressed interest in adopting, even in the absence of subsidies.[10] There are few if any adoptable children on the reserve, however, and she didn't know how to go about finding Indian children off-reserve or on other reserves who might be available. There are obviously problems with the mechanics of linking Indian children available for adoption with Indian families. It is not certain that the situation described by the social worker for the Bella Bella Band is common to other bands. Her comments, however, stand in contrast to statements often made by provincial child welfare authorities that they have trouble finding Indian families wanting to adopt.

A reduction in the number of Indian children placed for adoption in non-Indian homes may also be achieved if the practice of custom adoption is given legal sanction. As discussed in the previous chapter, custom adoptions are still common in at least parts of Canada. Yet only the Northwest Territories and Quebec provide for the legal recognition and sanction of custom adoption.[11]

A 1972 amendment to the Child Welfare Ordinance of the Northwest Territories gave preference to grandparents, where their home was judged suitable, in the adoption of a child.[12] A further amendment was added in 1973, primarily to expedite and facilitate custom adoptions. It allows the judge to waive some of the other provisions of the ordinance that impeded the formalization of such adoptions.[13] An order for adoption in the case of custom adoptions can now be given if a relatively simple affidavit is presented by the Department of Social Services.

Foster care is another area where significant improvement must be made. There is a need for more Native foster homes—but a greater need for child welfare authorities to take steps to bring this about.

The payment made to foster parents is one issue, in particular, that warrants review. One allegation often made is that there is sometimes a discrepancy between provincial foster care rates and the foster care payments provided by Indian Affairs to foster parents under their supervision. In both instances, there should be a review of the adequacy of the rates, given the economic position of many Native families. It may be, as Berger's commission suggested, that specialized foster care subsidies similar to adoption subsidies are necessary in order to increase the number of Native families able to foster.

An assessment of the methods used to recruit potential Native foster parents and foster homes for Native children must also be undertaken. The Alberta government, in an attempt to find more homes for Native children, recently sponsored a series of television commercials and was roundly criticized as a result. The three-minute slots were profiles of 25 permanent wards who were considered to have special needs because of physical, emotional or psychiatric problems. Several were Native children. The television shows generated a number a complaints from Native leaders. In a letter to the Minister of Social Services, the president of the Métis Association of Alberta asked, "Would you want to see your child advertised on television like a used car which is up for sale ?"[14]

The identification and selection of Native foster parents may be such a specialized activity that it demands approaches very different from those used to recruit non-Native foster parents. It may even require a different office or department of which the exclusive function would be the recruitment of Native foster parents.

Not only must recruitment methods be reviewed, but the criteria and standards used to determine the suitability of potential foster parents should be scrutinized. The issue of standards in the child welfare field has received a fair amount of attention in recent years. There is obviously a need for some sort of measure or gauge to ensure that children are placed in foster homes that will provide a safe, loving and healthy environment. However, any attempts to develop province-wide standards will be fraught with difficulties. The challenge is to develop a set of at least minimal standards that would have some meaning and offer some protection to children, but at the same time would be flexible enough to be adapted to the varying conditions and situations found at a community level. With respect to Native Peoples, the development of foster care standards must accommodate the unique cultural, social and spiritual values as well as the economic conditions common in many Native communities.

In 1981 Ontario's Ministry of Commmunity and Social Services released a consultation paper on proposed standards and guidelines to govern the placement of children in foster homes and the selection of foster parents. The 233-page document is an exhaustive and thorough review of an extremely complex issue.

Some of its proposals begin to address the unique needs of Native children, families and communities. In regard to the screening of requests for service or referrals, for example, the proposed standard that agencies would have to adhere to would demand that the request be answered in the language of the family needing assistance,[15] and that criteria for placing a child "include reference to... the child's cultural, racial, linguistic and social-economic background."[16]

There is even recognition that the physical appearance of the foster parent's home, which may be used to assess their suitability, is a relative factor. The document recommends as a guideline (that is, desirable but not mandatory) that "the foster home should be compatible with the norms of the local community, band or neighbourhood in maintenance and landscaping."[17]

Aside from a few references like those cited above, there is relatively little attention given to the need to consider the child's cultural background when placing him. This has the potential to affect children other than Native children as well, and is somewhat curious given that Ontario is now such a multicultural province. Certainly, the issue of culturally different approaches to child rearing has already been raised by some urban child welfare agencies, such as the Children's Aid Society of Metropolitan Toronto.

Ontario's standards for foster care, as well as those of all other provinces and territories, must also be evaluated to determine the extent to which they may preclude Native people as foster parents for economic reasons alone. Native people in all parts of Canada have complained that the physical standards relating to housing, safety, health, and so on are so stringent that, if rigidly applied, they would disqualify most Native people from fostering.

Perhaps the best way to illustrate this point is to refer to standards in an Indian community with its own child welfare program. An example is Fort Alexander, a relatively large reserve north-east of Winnipeg. The band has its own child and family service department, which supervises a number of foster homes located on the reserve. The department has established a variety of standards to which foster parents must adhere.[18] For example:

— if a water barrel is used, it must be tested and covered...
— if an outhouse is utilized, it must be maintained in sanitary condition.....

— the garbage must be disposed of or burnt....
— a phone should be installed, if possible....

These standards would not be appropriate in Vancouver or Winnipeg or Halifax where services like running water, garbage pick-up and telephones are taken for granted. By the same token, the standards used to choose foster parents in those three cities may be just as inappropriate if used at Fort Alexander. Any standards and guidelines for foster care must consider the economic circumstances of Native families and community norms. Clearly, the primary interest should be the capacity of foster parents to provide love, care and nurturing, regardless of their financial circumstances. Not only must we dispell the notion that poor people make poor parents, but we must ensure that warm, loving parents are not prevented from fostering because they are poor.

CHANGES IN PRACTICE AND PROCEDURE

As necessary and important as some of the changes proposed in the previous section are, they may still not be enough to reverse the disproportionate number of Native children taken into care. This fact was best expressed by a social worker in the Indian community of Sheshatshit in Labrador. She welcomed the amendments to Newfoundland and Labrador's Child Welfare Act that require that a child's culture be given consideration in determining his or her own best interests, but added, "However, I must say that I believe it is not the legislation which has prevented children from being removed ... but rather our own practice to find situations for children in the community."[19]

The practice of front-line workers can have a profoundly positive effect on mitigating some of the potential damage to Native children and families as a result of cultural misunderstanding. As a first step, front-line workers can and should be working to increase the involvement of Native Peoples in, and their understanding of, the child welfare system. This can be done in a variety of ways. For example, a supervisor with the Brant Children's Aid Society in southern Ontario actively encouraged residents of the Six Nations and New Credit reserves to take out memberships in the CAS. The residents of the reserves represent approximately 10 percent of the total population served by the Brant CAS but few members elected to its board were Indian. As a result of the membership drive, however, six of seven vacancies on the Brant board in 1982 were filled by residents of the reserves.[20]

Increased consultation with and involvement of Native Peoples with local child welfare workers is not limited only to those parts of the country with Children's Aid Societies however. A model employed in British Columbia can be used in juridictions where child welfare services are provided directly by provincial employees. The Stony Creek Reserve near Vanderhoof is one of several Indian communities in British Columbia that have established child welfare committees. The committee includes band councillors, elders and parents, as well as representatives of the Ministry of Human Resources and Indian Affairs. Its existence shifts the responsibility and some authority for addressing child welfare issues to residents of the reserve.

The Stony Creek Child Welfare committee is consulted before any apprehension of a child from the reserve and before plans are made for their children already in care. It can also appear as a "friend of the court" with respect to child welfare issues. Committee members may even become directly involved in assisting or counselling families in difficulty. The committee appears to be very successful. Within one year of its establishment, the rate of apprehension on the reserve decreased by 50 percent.[21] As a result, other reserves are following suit and attempts are being made to set up a district child welfare committee that would share information and resources between reserves.

The responsibility for informing and involving Native people in child welfare rests with all those in the system, however, and not only with front-line workers. Informational brochures and pamphlets, for example, should be available to Native people in their own language where numbers warrant. The Northwest Territories government already follows this practice and provides information about foster care and adoption in the Déné and Inuit languages.

Child welfare departments or agencies should be increasing their efforts to recruit Native foster homes. Attempts to increase the number of Native foster parents can succeed, as demonstrated by the Alberta Department of Social Services and Community Health. In 1975-76, Alberta's child welfare branch funded a foster home awareness and recruitment campaign by the Voice of Alberta Native Women's Society (VANWS). The campaign recruited well over 100 Native foster homes.[22] More recently, in 1982, Alberta officials approved a similar, limited campaign with two workers.[23]

The joint partnership between Alberta Social Services and the Voice of Alberta Native Women's Society suggests a whole range of other possibilities for improvement. An even better method, however, is to increase the participation of organizations of Native Peoples in the actual delivery of services to Native children and their family.

The past decade has seen a tremendous proliferation of organizations representing Native people. Some, like the National Indian Brotherhood (now the Assembly of First Nations), are essentially political bodies. Others, like Indian and Métis Friendship Centres, provide a variety of direct services to Native people in urban areas. There are still other single-purpose or single-issue Native organizations.

Many Native organizations are in a perfect position to provide services. They often have direct contact with Native people who are reluctant to become involved with non-Native organizations. They employ Native people who are more likely to be aware of and sensitive to cultural traits distinguishing Native from non-Native people. And they are in a much better position to plug into the Native people's network of family and community supports—unfamiliar territory for the majority of non-Native people.

There have already been some attempts to use Native organizations to deliver services. In Vancouver, the Indian Centre operates several group homes staffed by Native people for Native children. Their services are contracted by British Columbia's Ministry of Human Resources. In Alberta, a family courtworker program is operated by the Native Counselling Services of Alberta (NCSA). The program serves to strengthen the liaison between Native families, the courts and social agencies and, among other things, becomes involved in child welfare matters.

Of even greater potential is the recruitment of Native organizations to deliver prevention services designed to keep Native children from entering the child welfare system in the first place. Experimental projects of this type are in the developmental stage in several provinces.

In British Columbia a "crisis nursery" for Native children is being established in a region of Vancouver with a large Native population. It will be operated by Native parents and will provide care for children of newly arrived families until their parents secure employment and accomodation. In addition, it will provide temporary, emergency care for Native children without them formally being admitted into care.[24]

Saskatchewan Social Services is planning to contract with Native organizations to deliver a variety of prevention-oriented programs. Under consideration are a cultural camp for children of families on social assistance, an infant stimulation program for adolescent Native mothers whose infant children may be at risk, and recreational services and counselling for youth who have been in conflict with the law and their families.[25]

In New Brunswick, the Department of Social Services has entered into agreements with four reserves to provide a variety of personal social services in addition to, and supplementing, the basic child welfare program. Included would be such things as headstart programs and homemaker services.[26]

Native people, both individually and organizationally, are becoming more directly involved in the provision of primary and ancillary child welfare services. All of the evidence suggests that this trend is likely to continue. It also suggests that there is an immediate need to review and revamp educational and training programs for Native child welfare workers.

Some specialized programs already exist for Native people wanting to work in the social services. Several community colleges have a Native social service program. Some schools of social work have programs ostensibly designed for Native students. And the Saskatchewan Indian Federated College at the University of Regina is now graduating Native people with Bachelor of Social Work degrees.

The existing programs, however, cannot meet the immediate or future demand for trained Native workers. Futhermore, the quality and nature of some of these programs must be assessed. If the content and curriculum of social work courses are not substantially revised and adapted to Native values, beliefs and customs, their designation as Native programs has little meaning. In fact, it may be simply another method of assimilation.

The question of what constitutes an appropriate educational and training program for Native Peoples who are beginning to assume control of child welfare and other human service programs has never been seriously addressed. In fact, the question itself has only recently been posed. There is, however, an immediate need to look for answers. The University of Regina is one institution which is making the attempt through its recently developed Indian and Native Social Work Education Project.

While more Native people are likely to become involved in Native child welfare, there will continue to be many non-Native people working in the field. The training they receive is another area in which constructive changes are possible and necessary. Until very recently, there has been virtually no attempt made to sensitize non-Native social workers, child care workers, and foster or adoptive parents to the importance or implication of culture and background to Native children in their care. This was recognized in the report of the Berger royal commission in British Columbia and was the subject of several recommendations.[27]

This lack of cultural awareness and sensitivity in training programs was demonstrated more recently at the 1982 National Child Care Workers Conference in Banff. Approximately 25 child care workers from across the country participated in an intensive two-day workshop on child care and Native Peoples. The participants, none of whom were Native, worked in group homes, receiving and assessment centres, and juvenile detention centres where the vast majority of the children were Native. They shared a common belief that something about Native children distinguished them from non-Native children; the workers needed help in understanding why such differences existed if they were to have any positive impact on the Native children with whom they worked.[28]

It seems logical to suggest that the sentiment expressed by this group of child care workers probably reflects the feeling of many other non-Native people, whether child care workers, social workers or foster parents. There is an obvious need to provide an orientation and sensitization to Native culture and customs as part of the curriculum at universities, community colleges and even secondary and elementary schools. Similar programs need to be provided as part of in-service training for those already in the child welfare field who work with Native children. Alberta's Department of Social Services and Community Health is currently developing such a program.[29]

Notes to Chapter 5

[1]A tripartite review of the social services provided to Indian people in Ontario acknowledged this fact. Their report presented a conceptual model of the six transitional steps necessary to achieve an Indian-controlled social service system. These six steps would result in a system that was "Indian-determined, Indian-specific, Band controlled and Community based." See Technical Assistance and Planning Associates, Ltd., *Toward Indian Control of Indian Social Services* (Toronto, 1980).

[2]Family and Child Service Act, *Statutes of British Columbia* 1980, c. 11, s.12(2)(c).

[3]Correspondence from John Angus MacKenzie, Deputy Minister, Nova Scotia Department of Social Services, 21 October 1981.

[4]Child Welfare (Amendment) Act, 1972, *Statutes of Newfoundland* 1981, c. 54, s.3.

[5]Douglas Sanders, *Family Law and Native Peoples: Background Paper* (Ottawa: Law Reform Commission of Canada, 1975), p. 138.

[6]Ibid., p. 113.

[7]British Columbia Royal Commission on Family and Children's Law, *Tenth Report of the Royal Commission on Family and Children's Law: Native Families and the Law* (Vancouver, 1975), p. 36.

[8]Correspondence from Ross N. Findlater, Director of Child Welfare, Yukon Territory, 7 September 1982.

[9]British Columbia Royal Commission on Family and Children's Law, *Tenth Report,* p. 37.

[10]In conversation with the author, March 1982.

[11]Most of the material in this section has been taken from Sanders's work for the Law Reform Commission. See Sanders, *Family Law,* pp. 62-66; and Jack Sissons, *Judge of the Far North* (Toronto: McClelland and Stewart, 1968), pp. 142-45.

[12]Child Welfare Ordinance, *Revised Ordinances of the Northwest Territories,* c. 3, s.81(4), p. 116.

[13]Ibid., c. 3, s.79, p. 116.

[14]*Indian News* (Ottawa), December 1981, p. 8.

[15]Ontario, Ministry of Community and Social Services, *Foster Care: Proposed Standards and Guidelines for Agencies Placing Children* (Toronto, 1981), p. 32.

[16]Ibid., p. 45.

[17]Ibid., p. 118.

[18]In material received by the author during a visit to Fort Alexander, September 1981.

[19]Correspondence from Lyla MacEachern, Social Worker, Newfoundland and Labrador Department of Social Services, North West River, 16 November 1981.

[20]*Spectator* (Hamilton), 31 March 1982.

[21]Correspondence from David S. S. Marshall, British Columbia Ministry of Human Resources, 23 October 1981.

[22]Correspondence from Amelita A. Armit, Acting Assistant Deputy Minister, Planning Secretariat, Alberta Department of Social Services and Community Health, 13 May 1982.

[23]Correspondence from Susan Karamessines, Research Officer, Planning Secretariat, Alberta Department of Social Services and Community Health, 8 September 1982.

[24] British Columbia, Ministry of Human Resources, *Annual Report 1980-81*, p. 35.

[25] Correspondence from N. Duane Adams, Deputy Minister, Saskatchewan Social Services, 8 January 1982.

[26] Correspondence from R. A. Quigg, New Brunswick Department of Social Services, 10 November 1981.

[27] British Columbia Royal Commission on Family and Children's Law, *Tenth Report*, pp. 11, 34.

[28] In conversation with the author, May 1982.

[29] Correspondence from Amelia A. Armit, 13 May 1982.

CHAPTER 6
NEW INITIATIVES

The concern many Native people have about the damaging effects of the child welfare system on their families, communities and culture is not new. Efforts to actually do something about the problem are relatively recent, however, and are on the increase. There now exist several programs in different parts of the country designed specifically to resolve the problems discussed in this book. Most of these initiatives are fairly recent, and many are still at a developmental stage. The impetus behind many came primarily from Native people. In each case, they increase Native people's involvement in and responsibility for child welfare services provided to Native families—a prerequisite for constructive change and improvement.

The most significant of these projects will be discussed here, although this should not be considered an exhaustive list. These new initiatives vary in the extent of Native involvement and control, but reflect the different approaches being taken by Native and non-Native people in different regions to resolve a common problem. The programs fall into two distinct groups: those aimed at status Indians on-reserve and those geared towards Native people living off-reserve in a rural or urban setting, whether status or non-status Indian or Métis.

PROGRAMS ON-RESERVE

Spallumcheen Band

The example of the Spallumcheen Band is inevitably cited in any informed discussion of child welfare and Native Peoples. Located near Enderby, British Columbia the Spallumcheen Band has approximately 300 members. In 1980 the band council pased a by-law giving itself "exclusive jurisdiction over any child custody proceeding involving an

Indian child."[1] The band took this action when it was realized that 150 children had been removed from the reserve since the 1960s and placed in non-Indian homes. That represented virtually an entire generation and is a graphic example of the Sixties Scoop.

Officials at the Department of Indian Affairs initially rejected the by-law because, they claimed, they did not have the authority to delegate responsibility for child welfare. The by-law was submitted a second time, but was not formally disallowed. Even though Indian Affairs did not reject the by-law the second time around, they have made it clear that they do not accept its validity. Even the minister, John Munro, was prompted to state publicly that "although it has *not* been disallowed, the by-law would *not* stand up in court simply because nothing in the present Indian Act gives a Band Council or the Minister any power in the field of child welfare."[2]

The federal government, of course, was very concerned that it might be accused of condoning an action that was an infringement of provincial jurisdiction. British Columbia's Ministry of Human Resources, it must be remembered, has the responsibility to provide child welfare services on reserves by virtue of a long-standing, informal agreement with Indian Affairs. At the same time as the Spallumcheen Band was working to get approval for its by-law from officials in Ottawa, however, it was actively pursuing a plan that would defuse the federal argument about infringement on provincial jurisdiction.

On 16 October 1980, the chief of the Spallumcheen Band, Wayne Christian, signed an agreement with Grace McCarthy, British Columbia's minister of human resources. The agreement states:

> The Minister of Human Resources agrees to respect the authority of the Spallumcheen Band Council to assume responsibility and control over their own children. The Minister of Human Resources further agrees to the desirability of returning Indian children of the Spallumcheen Band presently in care of the Minister of Human Resources to the authority of the Spallumcheen Band and both parties agree to work out an appropriate plan in the best interests of each child presently in care, assuming that the Spallumcheen Band will develop necessary resources in negotiation with the federal government.[3]

It is no coincidence that the agreement was signed shortly after Chief Christian and others organized and led the Indian Child Caravan to Vancouver. Approximately 1,000 Indians converged at McCarthy's home on Thanksgiving Day, 1980, to protest the apprehension of Indian children from their families and reserves.

This chain of events had tremendous implications. The Spallumcheen Band is currently the only one in Canada having exclusive jurisdiction for the welfare of its children and operating completely outside the provincial sphere. Chief Christian argues that the bands authority to do so is vested in the sovereignty of Indian people.[4] As well, there now exists a by-law and an agreement with a provincial minister to support his argument.

The band has developed its own program with the help of some additional seed money from Indian Affairs. There don't appear to have been any major problems to date, although some difficulties are inevitable in any new program. The band members are more than aware, however, that their program is a test case watched closely by people all over the country. As a result, they are all the more determined to see it succeed.

The future of the Spallumcheen experiment may not be determined only by its success or quality. Its legal status is still up in the air. This is of particular concern to senior officials of the British Columbia government who believe they would be subject to a charge of dereliction of duty should anything happen to a child in care of the band or should the authority of the band ever be challenged in court.[5]

Regardless of the future, the very existence of the Spallumcheen program is tremendously significant. It reflects the concern all band members have about their children and their children's future. In part, it is a result of the personal commitment and talents of Chief Christian, who, like his brothers and sisters, was a victim of the Sixties Scoop.

While the example of the Spallumcheen Band is especially dramatic, it is not an isolated incident but reflects a growing preference for action rather than rhetoric. It provides the evidence that Native people are not simply talking about problems in child welfare, they are actively working to redress those problems.

Blackfoot Band

Another frequently mentioned program involves members of the Blackfoot Band of the Gleichen Reserve in Alberta. In 1975 a tripartite agreement was signed by Canada, Alberta and the Blackfoot Band. Under the terms of the agreement, the band administers the child welfare programs of the Child Welfare Branch of the Alberta Department of Social Services and Community Health.

Employees of the band's social services unit deliver services to band members living within the boundaries of the reserve. They include services relating to adoptions, child protection, foster homes, probation, and unwed mothers. The unit is administered by a mutually agreed-upon supervisor, who is provided by Alberta Social Services and Community Health. The supervisor is reponsible to the department to maintain standards and to the band council for day-to-day operations. The federal government pays 100 percent of the costs incurred by the program.

The Blackfoot agreement is significant in that it marks one of the first trilateral attempts to resolve the child welfare problem. While it obviously increases the direct involvement of Indian people in child welfare, the ultimate authority still rests with the province. The band provides the service—but under the supervision of a provincial employee and using provincial child welfare legislation. The mistrust some Indian people have of provincial programs and legislation may explain why this kind of agreement has not been extended to other reserves in Alberta. Nevertheless, the Blackfoot agreement was one of the first concrete efforts to increase in a meaningful way the participation of Indian people in the child welfare system.

The Canada-Manitoba-Indian Child Welfare Agreement

On 22 February 1982 representatives of the governments of Canada, Manitoba and the Four Nations Confederacy (FNC) signed an agreement that is perhaps the most comprehensive and significant development affecting the provision of child welfare services to Indian people. It is not simply a coincidence that this event took place in Manitoba. The disparity in the level and quality of child welfare services available to Indian children and families is more apparent in Manitoba than in other parts of Canada.

The cause of this disparity originated about 15 years ago. In 1966, an agreement was signed between the governments of Manitoba and Canada, resulting in extension of services of the Children's Aid Societies of western, central and eastern Manitoba to all reserves, involving 14 bands within their areas of jurisdiction. Indian Affairs reimbursed Manitoba for the cost of family services up to a stipulated amount, as well as for a per diem rate for maintenance of each child admitted to care.

Similar arrangements were not extended to the 45 bands in the rest of Manitoba, where child welfare services are provided directly by the province. In most cases, provincial child welfare services were made available only on an emergency basis and only in the case of extreme neglect. Any other assistance had to be provided by the staff of Indian Affairs or by band council employees, who had neither the mandate nor the training nor the resources to do an adequate job. As a result, little or no preventive, preparatory or follow-up work was done.

Since the 1966 agreement, some of the other bands have signed partial agreements resulting in partial services. Nevertheless, it is still the case in 1982 that bands in the northern part of the province do not have access to the range of child and family support services that has been provided to their southern counterparts for many years. It seems likely that this fact explains the significant involvement in the child welfare issue of the Four Nations Confederacy, which until recently was the political body representing almost all status Indians in Manitoba. It also helps to explain the establishment of the Manitoba Indian Child Welfare Subcommittee on 1 February 1977.

The subcommittee was a tripartite group comprising representatives of the Manitoba Indian Brotherhood (now the FNC), the government of Manitoba, and the government of Canada. Its mandate was to review the child welfare needs of Indian people and to develop plans and proposals. The report of the subcommittee was made public in March 1980 [6]

The Four Nations Confederacy's response[7] to the subcommittee's report called for the creation of 46 children's service worker positions at the band level and six resource positions at the tribal council level. (Tribal councils are groupings of individual bands.) These 52 positions would be in addition to the 15 child and family service positions already funded by Indian Affairs. The workers would be of Indian ancestry, would work on reserves, and would develop services based on traditional Indian beliefs, values and customs. It was recognized that the workers would have to undergo an intensive training program, but they would gradually begin to assume responsibility for providing child and family services. As bands developed their capacity to provide service, the province would transfer formal authority to tribal councils or groups of bands.

The February 1982 tripartite agreement—an outcome of the subcommittee's 1980 report, the FNC's response to it, and subsequent discussions—establishes the broad framework by which Indian communities in southern and central Manitoba will acquire authority and responsibility for child welfare.

It is essentially a master agreement, or an agreement in principle. The principles it enshrines will be put into practice only when subsidiary agreements have been signed that detail specific adminstrative and financial arrangements.

The intent of the agreement is that a full range of child welfare programs be provided for the participating Indian communities. Special emphasis will be given to programs and services that support Indian family life and prevent family breakdown and the removal of children. It is also intended to increase Indian participation in and responsibility and authority for child welfare.

The federal government will provide the funds to implement the agreement and will channel them directly to the agents delivering the service. The actual methods of service delivery may vary. Bands or tribal councils could apply for recognition as a separate autonomous child care agency, such as a Children's Aid Society. Or, they may choose to have the services provided directly by provincial officials with the involvement of the Indian community. Whatever the method used, the legislative basis for the provision of service is vested in the Manitoba Child Welfare Act—a provincial statute.

The master agreement is of tremendous significance. It is a comprehensive attempt to achieve an objective almost all Indian people share—increased authority for child welfare. In spite of this, some aspects of the agreement have been heavily criticized and may pose problems in the future.

In the first place, the agreement involves only slightly more than half the bands in the province. Twenty-four bands in northern Manitoba, where the child welfare situation has been most critical, broke away from the FNC in 1981 to form their own association known as the Manitoba Keewatinowi Okimakanak (MKO). In addition, some Indian people in Manitoba and elsewhere are suspicious of the master agreement. While it increases Indian responsibility for child welfare, the ultimate authority to do so is vested in provincial, not federal, legislation.

The suspicion of Indian people may very well be justified. Indian Affairs appears to have concentrated much more energy and committed much more money to resolving the Indian child welfare issue in Manitoba than in other provinces, such as Saskatchewan, where the situation is every bit as acute. Quite likely, the Manitoba agreement has been so strongly supported by Indian Affairs because it supports the federal position of gradual transference of responsibility to the provinces.

It is clear that federal officials are sincere in wanting to resolve the damage being done to Indian families, communities and culture by the existing provision of child welfare services. But they would also prefer to do so by supporting provincially mandated services rather than programs operated directly by Indian Affairs. The Manitoba agreement allows this and will invevitably be used by federal officials to support their argument that child welfare services for Indians are a provincial responsibility. It is a precedent that officials will undoubtedly attempt to extend to other jurisdictions.[8] As stated in the final paragraph of the press release announcing the signing of the agreement:

The spokesmen for the tripartite agreement heralded the new pact as a major new step in an important field and predicted positive beneficial results for Indian families and children. This tri-level approach, they said, could well extend nationwide.[9]

There is little likelihood that this approach will be extended nationwide once the implications of using provincial legislation are known and understood. In fact, it may never even be extended province-wide. The agreement's dependence on provincial legislation was the primary objection of the MKO.

The Dakota-Ojibway Child And Family Service

In a very real sense the future envisioned by the Canada-Manitoba-Indian Child Welfare Agreement is already here. It exists in the form of the Dakota-Ojibway Child and Family Service (DOCFS). On 1 July 1981 the authority for providing child welfare services to 8,500 members of eight Indian bands in southern Manitoba was officially transferred to the DOCFS. These bands were already linked into a political association known as the Dakota-Ojibway Tribal Council (DOTC). Previously, child welfare services had been delivered by three different Children's Aid Societies, those of western, eastern and central Manitoba.

The DOCFS was established by means of a separate arrangement between Canada, Manitoba and the DOTC that anticipated the master agreement. The formal transfer was accomplished by means of Section 7 of the Manitoba Child Welfare Act which permits the director of child welfare to vest a committee of "local citizens known to be interested in child welfare"[10] with the powers prescribed by the Act.

In effect, the DOCFS was Canada's first Indian children's aid society. It was developed by and is controlled and staffed by Indian people. The staff includes two supervisors, a foster home coordinator, and 16 child and family service workers, who live in the communities in which they work. Workers have exclusive responsibility for providing the full range of child welfare services, including family service and protection, child care, foster home placement, and supervision. Only adoption is still the responsibility of the CASs, but it will gradually be assigned to DOCFS.

The child and family service workers are guided and assisted by members of the local child welfare committee active on each reserve. The committee members serve in a voluntary capacity but may actually become directly involved in helping a family in difficulty. Each of the eight local committees delegate a representative to a regional child welfare committee. The regional committee makes the major service, financial and management decisions affecting the DOCFS and is analogous to a CAS board of directors. It administers a budget in excess of a million dollars, virtually all of which is transferred directly from Indian Affairs.

Fort Alexander Child and Family Service

The establishment of the DOCFS was not the first attempt made by Indian people in Manitoba to tackle the child welfare issue. In fact, it was predated by efforts of members of the Pas, Peguis and Fort Alexander Bands.

By 1974 the chief and council of the Fort Alexander Band were becoming increasingly concerned about the inadequacy of the social services available to resedents of their reserve. Child welfare was one of their primary concerns, and they blamed the inadequacy of services directly on the jurisdictional battle between Manitoba and the federal government. The province was reluctant to extend its child welfare program to residents of the reserve, and Indian Affairs argued that they did not have jurisdiction. This stalemate prompted Fort Alexander and several other bands to launch their own programs.

Under the direction of the chief and council, Fort Alexander proposed a model for its own child and family service program. It was designed to have a comprehensive and holistic approach —to protect the child, strengthen and support the family, and maintain and reflect traditional Indian beliefs, values and customs. It would also increase responsibility of all band members for child and family services. Initially, it was hoped that the program would include daycare, family life education social assistance, family counselling, foster homes, homemaker and other services.

On 3 November 1976 the band signed an agreement with Indian Affairs that provided for the funding to establish the child and family service program. The band was able to hire a trained social worker as the director and several Indian child and family workers. An agreement between the band and the School of Social Work at the University of Manitoba provided on-the-job training for the staff.

The program that has evolved is not as comprehensive as originally planned but does include foster care, homemaker services, social assistance, probation services, and counselling. More importantly it appears to be working.[11] As of September 1981, there were 45 children in care, all of whom were placed in foster homes on the reserve. Although that number seems high, it should be noted that Fort Alexander is a large reserve with approximately 2,000 residents. Only one child was living off the reserve, in an institution for the developmentally handicapped. Foster parents are paid according to the provincial scale.

The staff of four workers primarily recruit and supervise foster parents and provide individual and family support and counselling. They do not have the powers of apprehension, and two or three times a year they have to call in provincial child welfare officials to apprehend a child. The relationship with the local provincial community services office is good, however, and the recommendations made by the Fort Alexander staff with respect to a child's placement are usually respected.

As of 1982, the residents of Fort Alexander still do not have full control over their child welfare program. The ultimate responsibility rests with Manitoba's Department of Community Services and Corrections. The implications of the Canada-Manitoba-Indian Child Welfare Agreement for Fort Alexander remain to be seen, although the chief and council have consistently opposed the use of provincial laws in favour of federal Indian child welfare legislation.

Family and Children's Services of the District of Kenora

While not yet as advanced as the Fort Alexander program, a variety of pilot projects have been initiated several hundred miles to the east on reserves in the Kenora area of northwestern Ontario. They have been developed as part of the Ontario government's Native Child Welfare Prevention Program.

The Family and Children's Services of the District of Kenora, or the Kenora Children's Aid Society as it is more commonly called, serves a huge geographic area in northwestern Ontario. Approximately 85 percent of the children in its care are of Indian ancestry, although Native people comprise no more than 20 to 25 percent of the total population in the agency's catchment area.[12]

In response to these figures, the agency and several reserves submitted proposals to both the federal and provincial governments as early as 1972. They requested money to hire additional Indian staff who would work on-reserve to provide family support. It was not until 1979 that money was provided by the provincial government to initiate pilot projects. The objective of the pilot projects was to reduce the number of Indian children admitted into care by developing the capacity of certain Indian communities to protect and care for their children in their own milieu. Four reserves were initially identified to launch the experiments, with two other reserves being added later.

The development of each project was a long and difficult process involving extensive discussions between the CAS and the chief and councils of the reserves involved. Each community determined its own child welfare priorities and needs within the framework of the project. In most cases the bands chose to administer the child welfare project in its entirety. Funds are transferred to the band by the CAS, based on a budget negotiated by both parties. Staff of the CAS participated in the interviews for the child welfare workers, but the band made the final decision. The workers are employees of the band and accountable first to the band, then to the CAS.

The band workers are all involved in varying degrees in family support, crisis intervention, the locating of placement resources, and community education. A child welfare committee or the band council provides direction, consultation and support to individual workers. Band workers must also work with the regular CAS workers, of course, who still have the primary authority and responsibility for child welfare.

The Kenora experiments have developed slowly and not without some difficulties. Conflicts have arisen beween CAS workers and band workers or the reserve's child welfare committee. Some band workers have claimed that they are completely ignored by CAS workers.[13] In other instances, the band child welfare workers have been shunned by residents of reserves who view them as agents of the CAS "baby-snatchers." One worker has even been physically threatened.

It is essential to point out, however, that there is a degree of racial tension and hostility in Kenora that is greater than in many other communities. And there is certainly a great distrust by many Indian people of organizations like the CAS.

PROGRAMS OFF-RESERVE

Sheshatshit, Labrador

The history of the Sheshashit community in Labrador is a fascinating one and speaks volumes about the relationship between Native Peoples and the dominant society both past and present.[14] It is of particular relevance to this discussion because it is also the story of a very isolated, highly traditional Indian people and their experience with child welfare.

Sheshatshit is a community of approximately 600 Montagnais-Naskapi Indians, who call themselves Innu, meaning "people." It is a very young community; approximately 90 percent of the residents are under 30 years of age. It is also very poor. There are only 62 houses, which for the most part have no sewage system no running water and are heated by wood.

As it presently exists, the community of Sheshatshit is essentially a creation of non-Indian society. It has been referred to as an "enforced community."[15] Traditionaly, it was a summer resting place of the Montagnais-Naskapi, who were highly nomadic and whose travels were determined by the cycle of the caribou herds. In the 1950s the Roman Catholic church, the International Grenfell Association and the government decided that Sheshatshit should become a year-round settlement, so that the Montagnais-Naskapi children could attend school full time. On 1 April 1980 Sheshatshit was "made" a community in its own right. Previously, it had been considered a part of the community of North West River, across the river from Sheshatshit.

The residents of Sheshatshit are not status Indians in that they are not registered with Indian Affairs. This anomaly is the result of Newfoundland's late entry into Confederation. But neither are they non-status Indians, as they are entitled to be registered, a process which has been going on for several years. Consequently, Sheshatshit is not a reserve in the sense of other Indian communities.There is a band council that attempts to run local affairs, but as the result of a bilateral agreement between Newfoundland and Canada, its finances are controlled by a provincial government department.

The residents of Sheshatshit still follow a fairly traditional life style and many spend several months each year hunting and fishing inland. As much as a third of the village may be in the bush at any one time. Traditionally, it was the best or most experienced hunter who assumed the leadership role. In other words, the notion of an elected, centralized decision-making body has not developed from the experiences of the Montagnais-Naskapi. The band council, like the community itself, is a creation of non-Indian people.

This very brief description may serve to indicate how different Sheshatshit is from many of the other Indian communities described in this chapter. In their isolation the Montagnais-Naskapi have been able to retain their own culture and values more readily. For example, they still use their own language as the primary means of communicating.

With the development of a permanent community and the creation of a band council, the isolation of the Montagnais-Naskapi is gradually coming to an end. As the reach of the dominant society expands, Sheshatshit becomes host to two very different cultures attempting to accommodate each other. Child welfare is now an issue, and the approach being taken in Sheshatshit is unique to some extent. It may be instructive for those people in other very isolated Native communities.

During the past several years the involvement of the provincial department of social services in Sheshatshit, which falls within its jurisdiction, has changed a great deal. The department's responsibility used to consist of a visit once a week to distribute social assistance cheques. It has now expanded to include a district office situated in Sheshatshit with a staff of three, one of whom in Indian. Unlike the experience in many other Indian communities, the involvement of the provincial social services department in Sheshatshit appears to have been a positive one. Since the district office was established in 1979, for example, no children have been removed from the community.

For all intents and purposes, the community of Sheshatshit is now self-sufficient with respect to child welfare. Wherever possible, children in need of alternative care are placed with members of their extented family. Sometimes this has entailed ignoring official standards for the placement of children that were simply not appropriate to Sheshatshit. As the district social workers stated, there are other more important considerations: "Although children were placed in households already overcrowded and where the houses were in poor physical state, the children received the care they needed and did not have to be removed from the community."[16]

In cases where a child cannot be placed with an extended family member, he or she can still remain in the community in a group home that has been in operation for several years. The home has space for six children, and all of the staff are Indian people. The language of the house is Indian, and the activities are typical of those of other Sheshatshit households.

The positive developments in Sheshatshit have been, in part, the result of the feeling of some community members that it was important for their children to be cared for in their own community. To a large extent, these developments can also be attributed to the attitude and approach of the district office social workers.

The social workers in the Sheshatshit office have developed a close relationship with the residents of the community. They have demonstrated that their responsibility is to the community as much as, if not more than, to the department. And the notion of community responsibility and control is an underlying theme behind their efforts. As they have said:

> Indian people, as aboriginal people, have a right to have their services delivered by their own people, or at the very least in their own language....
>
> Our expectations should be as high for Indian peoples as for any person and therefore we have to recognize people as being capable of making decisions about their own lives. Therefore we believe that people should be allowed to learn from making their own mistakes.[17]

The experience of Sheshatshit is a significant one because it points out that non-Native people who are sensitive to the Native culture can, and should, work closely with Indian people, and that they can have a positive effect. They have a role to play in assisting Native people to find constructive means to resolve the child welfare issue in a way appropriate to the Native community.

Sandy Bay, Saskatchewan

Most of the projects discussed in this chapter pertain to status Indians on-reserve. Their development has been facilitated by the existence of a political structure with some degree of authority over a defined geographic area and with some discretionary control over finances. Non-status Indian and Métis communities do not always have an equivalent amount of autonomy, but constructive initiatives in child welfare are still possible. Sandy Bay is a case in point.

Located in northern Saskatchewan, Sandy Bay consists primarily of Métis and Cree Indians, both status and non-status. The provision of social services, inluding child welfare, is the responsibility of the province. In the late 1960s Sandy Bay was experiencing a variety of problems—inadequate housing, alcoholism, poor health, and so on. Many of these problems were exacerbated by the automation of a local power plant, which drastically increased the number of unemployed. Child welfare services were crisis-oriented. A worker flew into the community only several days each month, and there was virtually no preventive work done. The department's work primarily involved apprehension and resulted in children being removed from their community. Sandy Bay was considered to have one of the most serious child neglect problems in Saskatchewan.[18]

In 1968 child welfare officials were considering the establishment of an emergency child care facility in Sandy Bay. Before doing so, they held a series of discussions with community residents to discuss the desirability and feasibility of such a centre.

Initially, Sandy Bay residents were reluctant to participate. They were probably suspicious of the motives of provincial officials and, of course, language was a problem. Cree was the first language of many people in the community, and the discussions had to be translated. Gradually, however, a steering committee of community residents was established to plan the centre. Slowly and spontaneously, members of the committee became more directly involved in the welfare of Sandy Bay children. In the absence of a receiving home and with the approval of the child welfare department, the committee began to place children in private homes they had approved. Finally, one of their members was formally appointed a child welfare officer and vested with the powers and responsibility of the Child Welfare Act.

Sandy Bay eventually became virtually autonomous and self-sufficient with respect to child welfare. As the community took over the ownership of and responsibility for its child welfare program, more people became directly involved—and not only committee members. The effect was almost immediate and very positive. The number of children having to be removed from Sandy Bay was drastically reduced.

By 1980 Sandy Bay's child welfare program was still operating successfully. In fact, it spawned a variety of other community-based and controlled resources.[19] In addition to a foster home program and a 24 hour emergency child care facility staffed by Native people, Sandy Bay operated a daycare program and Oskietawin, a juvenile detention facility for Native youth 12-16 years of age. The community makes some of its facilities available to other northern communities but, more importantly, has set an example for others to emulate. At least one other northern Native community, Pinehouse, has developed its own child welfare program.

Vancouver Native Indian Child Welfare Advisory Committee

It is no coincidence that all of the programs described so far in this chapter have been developed in rural and/or remote settings. Relatively little attention has been devoted to developing alternative approaches in urban settings, where an increasing number of Indians and Métis are living. Concerns about Native child welfare are the same in the city, even though the solutions required may be very different.

A recent development in Vancouver suggests one positive and feasible approach to deal with the child welfare concerns of urban Natives. The impetus for the establishment of the Native Indian Child Welfare Advisory Committee came from Native people and social workers employed in Vancouver by the provincial Ministry of Human Resources (MHR). Both groups felt that needs of Native families and children were not adequately being met.

As originally conceived, the committee would consist of 15 Native people interested in and knowledgeable about the needs of Native children living in Vancouver. The committee would include one MHR staff person who would serve as a liaison between the committee and the ministry. Their involvement would be limited to the two service regions within the city of Vancouver which have a relatively large Native population.

The goals of the committee were threefold. First, it was hoped that the number of Native children removed from their families could be reduced. Second, if a child had to be removed, the committee was expected to help ensure that the child was placed in a suitable Native environment. Finally, the committee was intended to improve the capacity of the ministry to meet the needs of Native families in Vancouver.

The committee would meet its goals in variety of ways. It would provide advice and consultation to MHR and would become directly involved in case planning for Native children. It would assist in locating and developing Native placement resources and would also provide support to Native families in contact with MHR. The ultimate decision about a child would rest with MHR staff, of course, but in the event of disagreement with MHR, the committee could appear as a "friend of the court" and present its recommendation at a hearing.

The concept of a local Native child welfare committee was borrowed from the state of Washington and, in particular, the city of Seattle. Local advisory committees have existed in Washington for several years, and there is even a state-wide Native child welfare advisory committee.

The Vancouver committee is still in a developmental stage, but it is an urban model that can be used elswhere in Canada, whether child welfare services are delivered directly by provincial or territorial officials, or by organizations mandated by the government. It can address the concerns of all Native people, whether status or non-status Indian or Métis, without requiring a resolution of the jurisdictional issue or the necessity of new provincial legislation. And it can be implemented relatively simply and inexpensively. Most importantly, it is an approach that may benefit everyone, Native children and families as well as those in the child welfare field working with Native people.

Notes to Chapter 6

[1] Excerpts from the by-law are reprinted in Appendix C.
[2] Correspondence from Raymond S. Good, Special Assistant fo the Minister of Indian and Northern Affairs, 26 August 1981.
[3] Correspondence from David S. S. Marshall, British Columbia Ministry of Human Resources, 23 October 1981.
[4] In conversation with the author, September 1981.
[5] In conversation with the author, September 1981.
[6] Manitoba Tripartite Committee, *Report of the Indian Child Welfare Subcommittee—Manitoba* (Winnipeg, March 1980).
[7] Four Nations Confederacy, "Child and Family Services Proposal" (Winnipeg, September 1980).
[8] In the Summer of 1982, in conversation with the author an official of the Department of Indian Affairs predicted that an agreement similar to and modelled after the Manitoba arrangement would soon be implemented in New Brunswick.
[9] Joint press release issued by the governments of Canada and Manitoba, and the Four Nations Confederacy, 22 February 1982, in Winnipeg.
[10] Child Welfare Act, *Statutes of Manitoba* 1974, c. 30, s. 7.
[11] The information in this section was provided to the author during a conversation with Bert Crocker and Lillian and Lawrence Morriseau at Fort Alexander, September 1981.
[12] Information contained in correspondence received from Margie Cressman, Kenora CAS, 4 August 1981.
[13] In conversation with the author, September 1981.
[14] All of the material in this section has been drawn from Lyla

MacEachern and Peter Bown, Untitled paper presented to the Canadian Rural Social Work Forum, Lakehead University, Thunder Bay, Ontario, 25-27 May 1981.

[15]Ibid., p. 4.

[16]Ibid., p. 9.

[17]Ibid., p. 6.

[18]For a more detailed discussion of the developments in Sandy Bay, see Len Soiseth, "A Community that Cares for Children" *Canadian Welfare*, vol. 46, no. 3 (May/June 1970).

[19]These and other examples of Sandy Bay's success with social and economic community development are the subject of a half hour documentary film entitled *We Can*. The film was produced by the Faculty of Social Work at the University of Regina with financial assistance from the Donner Canadian Foundation.

CHAPTER 7
THE SHAPE OF THINGS TO COME

While child welfare for Native Peoples cannot be said to be an issue that has a great impact on the national consciousness, there is reason to believe that it will receive increased attention in the coming years for at least two reasons.

In the first place, the Indian population has increased at a faster rate than the general population for many years.[1] In some provinces, Native people constitute the largest minority group and Native political parties are beginning to emerge, as evidenced in the 1982 Saskatchewan election. In some prairie cities, Native people may soon comprise 20 to 25 percent of the total population.

An additional factor may also spur an interest in this issue. The severe recession of the early 1980s will inevitably force an analysis of government costs in an attempt to reduce expenditures. The cost of maintaining children outside of their family unit is very high, and it may not be long before fiscal conservatives realize that not only are there a disproportionate number of Native children in care, but they incur a disproportionate amount of the cost. The call for a review of the welfare system by those concerned about the effects on Native children and families may be joined and, ironically, strengthened by those who are primarily concerned about the cost.

The story behind the statistics presented in this book is a depressing one. Obviously, some Native children have needed and benefitted from the asssistance provided by child welfare programs. But many, too many, have suffered. The damage done has been extensive. Many Native children have suffered psychologically from their involvement in the child welfare system. The experience has increased their sense of alienation and the degree of confusion about their personal and cultural identity. Some have suffered even more. It is no exaggeration to suggest that some Native children have died, either through neglect because the help their families needed was not available or by their own hands because of the inadequacy of assistance that was provided.

Children have not been the only victims. It is a bitter irony that a system that is designed to protect children and support families has served to weaken Native family life inestimably. And, in so doing, because the family had traditionally been the primary social unit in Native communities, it has also damaged a distinct way of life.

In the long run, all Canadians suffer for the disproportionate representation of Native children in the child welfare system. The disproportionately high incarceration rate of Native people in prisons and jails is not an unrelated coincidence. Many consider the child welfare system to be a kind of training ground for children who "graduate" to the juvenile justice system and, finally, to the penal system. Society as a whole pays the price, not only in human terms because of a waste of human potential, but in financial terms.

It is important to bear in mind that the situation that exists today, to a large extent, is the result of attitudes, beliefs and practices in vogue 15, 20 and even 30 years ago. Many of those attitudes, fortunately, have changed, but not all. One such example was described by a teacher in a juvenile detention facility with a large Native population.[2] One of the residents, who had received permission to talk to his parents by telephone, began speaking his Native language. The child care worker who was present immediately pulled the phone from the boy's hand and ordered him to "speak English." Obviously, the message given this boy is the same as that delivered to children in the old Indian residential schools who were physically punished for speaking their own language.

A middle-aged man who taught in the same facility provided another example. As much as he wanted to, he admitted that he could not get over his feeling that Native people were inferior. Born and raised in a small western town, this notion had been instilled in him and reinforced from the time he was a child. Even though he no longer believed it, he knew that this attitude probably affected his relationship to the Native children he taught.

The examples above have been cited only to emphasize the fact that old attitudes die hard. We cannot wait to address the problems in child welfare that confront Native Peoples until Canadians as a whole become more tolerant and less biased. Hopefully, that is happening, but it will never be the panacea for the difficulties described here.

As bleak as the current situation may be, there is no cause for despair. In fact, there is much room for optimism. That is, perhaps, the most important message to everyone concerned about this issue. From Spallumcheen to Sandy Bay to Sheshatshit, there is a growing list of serious and constructive attempts to mitigate the flaws in child-welfare that adversely affect Native children and families. Increasingly, Native people are demonstrating their preference for action over rhetoric. And, as they succeed, the sense of self-worth and confidence of Native Peoples in their own abilities is infused and reinforced both individually and collectively.

The increasing activity at a grass-roots level is resulting in more serious attention being paid to the issue at the political level. More Native political organizations are devoting more of their resources to the child welfare problem. For example, a two-day workshop was sponsored in April 1982 by the Four Nations Confederacy and the National Indian Brotherhood (shortly thereafter restructured and renamed the Assembly of First Nations ⌐AFN⌐). Representatives of most provincial and territorial organizations of status Indians discussed the problem from their own perspective and agreed on the need for a clear, concise position by the AFN. A task force was struck to continue the work begun at the workshop.

Provincial government officials also appear to be taking the issue more seriously. In March 1981 the Alberta Ombudsman released the report of his investigation into the province's foster care program. During the course of his work, a special emphasis was placed on the needs of Native children. The provision of child welfare service to Native families in Alberta will probably also be addressed as part of a broader review headed by the Honourable Mr. Justice Cavanaugh. Appointed in March 1980 by the lieutenant-governor-in-council, the Cavanaugh Commission of Inquiry is to examine and report on all aspects of Alberta's Child Welfare Act and the Social Care Facilities Licensing Act.

More recently, in March 1982, Manitoba's minister of community services and corrections announced the establishment of a committee designed to review the placement procedures involving Native children, with particular emphasis on foster home and adoption placements. Headed by Judge E. C. Kimelman of the Family Division of the Provincial Judges Court, the committee was established after Manitoba instituted a moratorium on the placement of Native children in the United States.

Although the initiatives discussed here provide reason for optimism, there are a number of other issues that must be addressed much more thoroughly if all of the shortcomings in Native child welfare are to be overcome and not repeated in the future.

Perhaps the most important is the situation of urban Natives, whether status or non-status Indian or Métis. The majority of the initiatives in Native child welfare are taking place at a reserve level—but what of the 28 percent of status Indian children living off-reserves? Many of them live in urban centres, as do many non-status Indian and Métis children. The concerns off-reserve are the same, but the solutions are very different from those that can be implemented on a reserve. There is obviously a need to devote more attention to their child welfare needs.

Another issue warranting careful consideration concerns Inuit children and families. With such changes as the rapid development in the north and an increase in the average number of children in each family, the traditional Inuit customs, values and traditions are being severly tested. It is not yet known whether Inuit families and children will experience problems similar to those of other Native groups in regard to child welfare.

Richard Harrington, who has travelled extensively throughout the Arctic, recently wrote, "Inuit children, in my experience have the most harmonious upbringing in the world."[3] As contact between the Inuit and the dominant culture increases, as it inevitably will, we must ensure that, with the best of intentions, we do not upset that harmony.

In addition to emerging issues, there are barriers currently in existence that may continue to impede efforts to overcome some of the problems described in previous chapters. One of these barriers has been erected by Native people themselves and, in particular, by Native leaders. The child welfare issue has not received a high priorty on the agenda of Native leaders. Their attention has been focussed on the constitution, land claims, and economic development. When they have dealt with the child welfare issue, it was usually in response to the concerns expressed by other Native groups, especially Native women's associations. Although this appears to be changing, Native leaders in the past, with some notable exceptions, have been more prone to rhetoric than action when addressing the child welfare problem. In this respect, Native politicians are not so different from their provincial and federal counterparts.

More disturbing is the fact that this lack of attention to child welfare and other social service issues in not always an oversight. In some cases, it seems to be a deliberate strategy best summed up as the notion that social development follows economic development. It is argued that the limited resources of Native leaders should be directed primarily at improving the economic position of Native Peoples. Only then will social problems be overcome.

This attitude was expressed in an editorial in *New Breed*, a monthly magazine published by the Association of Métis and Non-Status

Indians of Saskatchewan (AMNSIS). The editorial, which had foster care and adoption as its subject, concluded by stating:

This is why AMNSIS and other Native groups in Saskatchewan and Canada continue in the struggle for the settlement of aboriginal rights and land claims, for economic independence, and for equal opportunity. Not until the root of the problem is solved, will the social problems being faced by Native people and their children start to decrease.[4]

Although the editor was stating a personal opinion and not necessarily the positon of AMNSIS, the sentiment contained in that paragraph does reflect the beliefs of some Native leaders.

No one can argue that it is not important to invest much time and effort into improving the economic situation of Native people. But to do so without also paying serious attention to issues of social development is shortsighted. Many of the problems Native people experience with child welfare are not a result of their economic situation. And, conversely, an improvement in their financial position will not solve all social problems. Efforts at economic development and social development must go hand in hand. Successes achieved by Native people in economic development will prove futile if there is no future generation to benefit from them.

Improvements in child welfare that will be beneficial to Native people may also be stymied by another barrier, one that confronts everyone who attempts social change. Large, institutionalized systems are inherently resistant to change—even changes that are desirable.

As an example, some people are concerned about developments in Manitoba—particularly, the establishment of agencies like the Dakota-Ojibway Child and Family Service. This concern reflects a belief that the development of a separate authority serving only the Native child has the potential for discrimination. Others suggest that the emergence of a distinct and parallel child welfare system, which is the inevitable result, wil prove inefficient, cumbersome and costly. While those expressing such concerns are no doubt sincere, they ignore the fact that parallel child welfare systems have operated in the past and still do in some jurisdictions. Toronto, for example, has three distinct child welfare organizations defined by religion: one serves Catholic families, one serves Jewish families, and the third, all others.

While the system's resistance to change presents a challenge, another potential barrier may actually threaten attempts to improve child welfare services to Native Peoples. More and more people are coming to believe a potential backlash against Native people will manifest itself in a few years.

The process of settling land claims has been going on for many years. This issue will likely receive increased attention from the Canadian public as a result of the constitutional conference in 1983 to define aboriginal and treaty rights. Hopefully, by the end of this decade, many outstanding claims will be settled. But the cost is likely to be tremendous, and ultimately, it is the Canadian taxpayer who will foot the bill. A response from the non-Native public appears inevitable, and it may not be very pleasant. As settlements are reached, many of the old stereotypes about Native people may be expressed once again. As well, there will be increased attention paid to any other measures primarily of benefit to Native people—especially those for which there is a cost.

In reaction, many questions are likely to be posed about the position of Native people in Canadian society. Some may ask whether or not it is just to treat Native people differently from other cultural minorities. Does it threaten the image of Canada as a just and multicultural society where everyone is treated equally regardless of where in the world they originated? Is it reasonable to even entertain the notion of a unique Native community distinct from but still a part of the Canadian polity?

Many of these questions were considered during the inquiry into the Mackenzie Valley Pipeline conducted by Mr. Justice Thomas Berger. A small excerpt from Berger's report provides perhaps the only possible rejoinder. Although he refers to the Déné and Inuit, his comments apply equally to other Native Peoples:

> Why should the native people of Canada be given special consideration? No such consideration has been offered to the Ukrainians, the Swedes, the Italians, or any other race, ethnic group or nationality since Confederation. Why should the native people be allowed political institutions of their own under the Constitution of Canada, when other groups are not?
>
> The answer is simple enough: the native people of the North did not immigrate to Canada as individuals or families expecting to assimilate. Immigrants chose to come and to submit to the Canadian polity; their choices were individual choices. The Déné and the Inuit were already here, and were forced to submit to the polity imposed upon them. They were

here and had their own languages, cultures and histories before the arrival of the French or English. They are the original peoples of Northern Canada. The North was—and is—their homeland.[5]

As northern Canada is the homeland of the Déné and Inuit, Canada in its entirety is the only homeland known to Indian, Métis and Inuit peoples. This simple fact must not be lost to us as we address child welfare or any other issue affecting Native Peoples.

The potential backlash against Native Peoples, the system's inertia, and differing priorities of Native leaders are a few of the predictable factors that will influence the child welfare system of the future as it impacts on Native families and children. There is, however, a somewhat unpredictable factor of equal if not more importance.

The process of revising and ultimately patriating the Canadian constitution in 1982 has profound implications for the future of Canadian society. The Charter of Rights may be of particular importance. Native Peoples, however, are likely to be affected by the existence of the charter more than any other Canadians.

The Charter of Rights in the Constitution Act, 1981, contains a provision which recognizes the rights of Native Peoples. The key section 35 reads: "The existing aboriginal and treaty rights of the aboriginal peoples of Canada are hereby recognized and affirmed."[6]

Section 37 of the charter requires that a constitutional conference of first ministers be convened within a year of the constitution's patriation to define the term "existing aboriginal and treaty rights."[7] Representatives of Indian, Métis and Inuit peoples will be invited to participate in the discussions.

These two sections are of tremendous significance. They enshrine in the constitution the notion that Native Peoples have certain unique rights by virtue of being the aboriginal peoples of Canada. Just as important, it is spelled out subsequently that the Métis and Inuit as well as the Indian peoples are considered to have such rights. Furthermore, a meeting with the status of a constitutional conference is mandatory in order to define such rights.

The redefinition of the rights of Native Peoples has already begun to alter their positon in Canadian society. This has even started to have an effect on the provison of child welfare services. As one provincial assistant deputy minister of social services said in the summer of 1982, "The impact of constitutional changes on Native Peoples in Canada requires a continual examination of the ministry's policies and practices."[8]

129

There is a every reason to believe that the issue of child welfare services for Native Peoples may equally be affected by the dicussions at the constitutional conference in the spring of 1983. By October 1982 several items had already been discussed for inclusion on the agenda. One of the agenda items will likely concern the delivery of services by the federal and provincial governments, and it seems likely that child welfare will figure in that discussion. It is no exaggeration to say that the constitutional conference of 1983 may offer the best chance of resolving the jurisdictional difficulties affecting child welfare described here.

In the final analysis, the subject of this book is not simply a child welfare matter, it is also a political issue. It has as much to do with federal-provincial relations and the division of power between both those levels of government and Native Peoples. Often, in such tussles for power, certain individuals suffer as a result. In this case, it happens to be that segment of the population with the least amount of power and no voice—children, who also happen to be Native.

As unjust as it may seem, the influence of politics and power on child welfare is undeniable. The issue presents formidable difficulties for those attempting to find solutions. It also requires more effort and the development of more creative strategies. And it demands a collective effort. There is little to be gained in pointing fingers and laying the blame on others. The problem is now understood, as are many of the possible solutions. All of us, Native and non-Native, will be deserving of blame in the future, however, if we fail to continue with and to augment our efforts to find solutions to the problems described in this book. The future welfare of Native children is in our hands.

Notes to Chapter 7

[1] For a discussion of Indian demographics, see Canada, Department of Indian and Northern Affairs, *Indian Conditions: A Survey* (Ottawa, 1980), p. 8; and J. Rick Ponting and Roger Gibbins, *Out of Irrelevance: A Socio-Political Introduction to Indian Affairs in Canada* (Toronto: Butterworths, 1980), pp. 37-43.

[2] In conversation with the author, May 1982.

[3] Richard Harrington, *The Inuit: Life as It Was* (Edmonton: Hurtig, 1981).

[4] "The Leaders of Tomorrow," *New Breed*, vol. 12, no. 9 (September 1981).

[5]Mr. Justice Thomas R. Berger, *Northern Frontier, Northern Homeland* and: *The Report of the Mackenzie Valley Pipeline Inquiry,* vol. I (Ottawa: Canada Department of Supply and Services, 1977), p. 173.

[6]Canada, *House of Commons Debates,* Ottawa: vol. 124, no. 268, 1st Session, 32nd Parliament, p. 13642.

[7]Ibid., p. 13643.

[8]Correspondence to the author, July 1982.

APPENDIX A

QUESTIONNAIRE

The following detailed and very specific set of questions was sent to all provincial and territorial deputy ministers of social services to assist in the compilation of this report.

1. Does your department presently have an agreement or agreements with the federal government to provide child welfare services to status Indians living *on-reserve*? If so, what are the elements and conditions of the agreement?

2. If such an agreement exists, what services are provided and what proportion of the cost of such services is borne by your department and what proportion by the federal government?

3. If no such agreement exists, are there instances where officials of your department may provide child welfare services to status Indians living *on-reserve*? If so, under what circumstances would such services be provided? Which level of government would bear the cost of such services?

4. Does your department presently provide child welfare services to Inuit families living in your province or territory? If so, are such services provided by agreement with the federal government and what are the conditions, financial and otherwise, of such an agreement?

5. Does your department provide child welfare services to status Indians living *off-reserve*? Are such services provided by way of an agreement with the federal government? If yes, what are the conditions, financial and otherwise, of the agreement?

6. If no agreement exists, are child welfare services provided on the same basis to status Indians living *off-reserve* as they are to non-Indian residents of your province or territory? Please explain any differences which may exist.

7. Are there any discussions ongoing or planned between your province or territory and the federal government which may substantially alter any of the responses you have provided to the above questions? If so, please explain.

8. Are the full range of child welfare services offered by your department available to non-status Indian and Métis familes? If not, please explain.

9. Has your department implemented or is it planning to implement any programs to accommodate what are considered to be the specialized child welfare needs of Native families whether status or non-status Indian, Métis or Inuit? If so, could you briefly provide details of such programs, including the nature and extent of involvement of Natives in their planning and delivery.

10. Do existing child welfare legislation and regulations in your province or territory contain any special provisions to accommodate what are considered to be the specialized needs of Native families? Are amendments of this nature being planned? Please provide the details of such provisions — existing or planned.

11. Does legislation exist in your province or territory which prohibits the placement of Native children in foster or adoption homes ouside of Canada? If not, how many Native children have been placed ouside of Canada in each of the last ten years and where?

12. Would you please provide the following statistical information for *each* of the last five years. In addition, wherever possible, would you report the figures for Native children by the categories: (1) status Indian, (2) non-status Indian, (3) Métis, or (4) Inuit.

- the total number of children "in care" and an explanation of how that figure is derived
- the number of Native children "in care"
- the total number of children placed in foster homes
- the number of Native children placed in (i) Native foster homes and (ii) non-Native foster homes
- the number of Native foster homes
- the total number of children placed for adoption
- the total number of Native children placed for adoption with (i) Native families, and (ii) non-Native families
- a breakdown of the reasons children were admitted into care for (i) the total "in care" population, and (ii) the Native "in care" population

- the wardship status by number of (i) all children "in care," and (ii) all Native children "in care"
- the number of (i) all children "in care" who were returned to their parents, and (ii) Native children "in care" who were returned to their parents

APPENDIX B

EXCERPTS FROM THE UNITED STATES
INDIAN CHILD WELFARE ACT

Public Law 95-608—Nov. 8, 1978   92 Stat. 3069

Public Law 95-608
95th Congress

An Act

To establish standards for the placement of Indian children in foster or adoptive homes, to prevent the breakup of Indian families, and for other purposes.

Be it enacted by the Senate and House of Representatives of the United States of America in Congress assembled, that this Act may be cited as the "Indian Child Welfare Act of 1978."

Sec. 2.   Recognizing the Special relationship between the United States and the Indian tribes and their members and the federal responsibility to Indian people, the Congress finds—

. . .

(4)   that an alarmingly high percentage of Indian families are broken up by the removal, often unwarranted, of their children from them by nontribal public and private agencies and that an alarmingly high percentage of such children are placed in non-Indian foster and adoptive homes and institutions;
(5)   that the States, exercising their recongnized jurisdiction over Indian child custody proceedings through administrative and judicial bodies, have often failed to recognize the essential tribal relations of Indian people and the cultural and social standards prevailing in Indian communities and families.

. . .

TITLE I—CHILD CUSTODY PROCEEDINGS

Sec. 101 (a)   An Indian tribe shall have jurisdiction exclusive as to any State over any child custody proceeding involving an Indian child who resides or is domiciled within the reservation of such tribe, except where such jurisdiction is otherwise vested in the State by existing Federal law. Where an Indian child is a ward of a tribal court, the Indian tribe shall retain exclusive jurisdiction, notwithstanding the residence or domicile of the child.

(b)   In any State court proceeding for the foster care placement of, or termination of parental rights to, an Indian child not domiciled or residing within the reservation of the Indian child's tribe, the court, in the absence of good cause to the contrary, shall transfer such proceeding to the jurisdiction of the tribe, absent objection by either parent, upon the petition of either parent or the Indian custodian or the Indian child's tribe, provided, that such transfer shall be subject to declination by the tribal court of such tribe.

(c)   In any State court proceeding for the foster care placement of, or termination of parental rights to, an Indian child, the Indian custodian of the child and the Indian child's tribe shall have a right to intervene at any point in the proceeding.

. . .

Sec. 105 (a)   In any adoptive placement of an Indian child under State law, a preference shall be given, in the absence of good cause to the contrary, to a placement with (1) a member of the child's extended family; (2) other members of the Indian child's tribe; or (3) other Indian families.

(b)   Any child accepted for foster care or preadoptive placement shall be placed in the least restrictive setting which most approximates a family and in which his special needs, if any, may be met. The child shall also be placed with reasonable proximity to his or her home, taking into account any special needs of the child. In any foster care or preadoptive placement, a preference shall be given, in the absence of good cause to the contrary, to a placement with

(i) a member of the Indian child's extended family;
(ii) a foster home licensed, approved, or specified by the Indian child's tribe;
(iii) an Indian foster home licensed or approved by an authorized non-Indian licensing authority; or

(iv) an institution for children approved by an Indian tribe or operated by an Indian organization which has a program suitable to meet the Indian child's needs.

(c)   In the case of a placement under subsection (a) or (b) of this section; if the Indian child's tribe shall establish a different order of preference by resolution, the agency or court effecting the placement shall follow such order so long as the placement is the least restrictive setting appropriate to the particular needs of the child, as provided in subsection (b) of this section. Where appropriate, the preference of the Indian child or parent shall be considered; provided, that where a consenting parent evidences a desire for anonymity, the court or agency shall give weight to such desire in applying the preferences.

(d)   The standards to be applied in meeting the preference requirements of this section shall be the prevailing social and cultural standards of the Indian community in which the parent or extended family resides or with which the parent or extended family members maintain social and cultural ties.

. . .

Sec. 107 Upon application by an Indian individual who has reached the age of eighteen and who was the subject of an adoptive placement, the court which entered the final decrees shall inform such individual of the tribal affiliation, if any, of the individual's biological parents and provide such other information as may be necessary to protect any rights flowing from the individual's tribal relationship.

TITLE II—INDIAN CHILD AND FAMILY PROGRAMS

Sec. 201 (a)   The Secretary is authorized to make grants to Indian tribes and organizations in the establishment and operation of Indian child and family service programs on or near reservations and in the preparation and implementation of child welfare codes. The objective of every Indian child and family service program shall be to prevent the breakup of Indian families and, in particular, to insure that the permanent removal of an Indian child from the custody of his parent or Indian custodian shall be a last resort.

APPENDIX C

EXCERPTS FROM
SPALLUMCHEEN INDIAN BAND BY-LAW
NO. 2-1980

1. RECOGNIZING the special relationship which exists among band members to care for each other and to govern themselves in accordance with the five basic principles of Indian government:

(i) WE ARE THE ORIGINAL PEOPLE OF THIS LAND AND HAVE THE ABSOLUTE RIGHTS TO SELF-DETERMINATION THROUGH OUR OWN UNIQUE FORMS OF INDIAN GOVERNMENTS (BAND COUNCILS).

(ii) OUR ABORIGINAL RIGHT TO SELF-DETERMINATION THROUGH OUR OWN UNIQUE FORMS OF INDIAN GOVERNMENTS ARE TO BE CONFIRMED, STRENGTHENED AND EXPANDED OR INCREASED, THROUGH SECTION 91(24) OF THE BRITISH NORTH AMERICA ACT.

(iii) OUR INDIAN RESERVE LANDS ARE TO BE EXPANDED TO A SIZE THAT IS LARGE ENOUGH TO PROVIDE FOR THE ESSENTIAL NEEDS OF ALL OUR PEOPLE.

(iv) ADEQUATE AMOUNTS OF LAND, WATER, FORESTRY, MINERALS, OILS, GAS, WILDLIFE, FISH AND FINANCIAL RESOURCES ARE TO BE MADE AVAILABLE TO OUR INDIAN GOVERNMENTS ON A CONTINUING BASIS AND IN SUFFICIENT QUANTITIES TO ENSURE DOMESTIC, SOCIO-ECONOMIC, SELF-DETERMINATION FOR PEACE, ORDER AND GOOD GOVERNMENT OF INDIAN PEOPLE.

(v) OUR INDIAN GOVERNMENTS (BAND COUNCILS) OR LEGISLATURES ARE TO HAVE THE AUTHORITY TO GOVERN THROUGH MAKING LAWS IN RELATION TO MATTERS COMING WITHIN SPECIFIED AREAS OF JURISDICTION THAT HAVE BEEN DEFINED BY OUR PEOPLE.

AND RECOGNIZING OUR AUTHORITY TO CARE FOR OUR CHILDREN WITHIN THE TERMS OF THE *INDIAN ACT* R.S.O. 149 S. 81

The Spallumcheen Indian Band finds:

(a) that there is no resource that is more vital to the continued existence and integrity of the Indian Band than our children.

(b) that an alarmingly high percentage of Indian families are broken up by the removal, often unwarranted, of their children from them by non-band agencies.

(c) that the removal of our children by non-band agencies and the treatment of the children while under the authority of non-band agencies has too often hurt our children emotionally and serves to fracture the strength of our community, thereby contributing to social breakdown and disorder within our reserve.

2.   In this by-law, unless the context otherwise requires:

. . .

"Extended Family Member" shall be defined by the law and custom of the Spallumcheen Indian Band and shall be a person who is the Indian child's grandparent, aunt or uncle, brother or sister, brother-in-law or a sister-in-law, niece or nephew, first or second cousin or step-parent.

"Family" means the unit within which the Indian child is a permanent member and usually resides.

"Indian Custodian" means any person who has legal custody of an Indian child under custom or under this by-law or whose temporary physical care, custody and control has been transferred by the parent of such child.

"Parent" means any biological parent or parents of an Indian child or any Indian person who has lawfully adopted an Indian child, including adoptions under tribal law or custom.

. . .

"Child Custody Proceeding" shall mean and include:

(a) any action relocating an Indian child from the home of his/her parents, extended family member, or Indian custodian placement in another home.

(b) and the maintenance of the Indian child in the home of the Indian custodian.

(c) and the return of the Indian child to the home of the Indian child's family.

3. (a) The Spallumcheen Indian Band shall have exclusive jurisdiction over any child custody proceeding involving an Indian child, notwithstanding the residence of the child.

(b) The Provincial Court shall transfer proceedings to the jurisdiction of the Indian Band where the proceedings involve the placement of an Indian child or the termination of parental rights to an Indian child.

4. (a) The Band Council shall see that the Provisions of this by-law are carried out and may exercise such powers as are necessary to carry out this by-law including:—

(b) The Appointment of such persons to act on behalf of the Band Council in the performance of any of the duties under this by-law as the occasion may require, and

(c) The making of such regulations as, from time to time may be necessary to carry out the provisions of this by-law including but not limiting regulations:

(i) governing the creation of special programs designed to aid in any child custody proceeding and in fulfilling the purposes of this by-law.

(ii) governing the expenditure of band money designed to aid in any child custody proceeding and fulfilling the purposes of this by-law.

(iii) governing the conduct of Indian children, Indian guardians, parents, or extended family members, or any person acting on behalf of any band member in a child custody proceeding which may be necessary for the proper working of this by-law.

5. The Chief and Council shall be the legal guardian of the Indian child, who is taken into the care of the Indian Band.

6. The Chief and Council and every person authorized by the Chief and Council may remove an Indian child from the home where the child is living and bring the child into the care of the Indian Band, when the Indian child is in need of protection.

7. An Indian Child is in need of protection when:

(a) a parent, extended family member or Indian guardian asks the Indian Band to take care of the child;

(b) the child is in a condition of abuse or neglect endangering the child's health or well-being, or

(c) the child is abandoned, or

(d) the child is deprived of necessary care because of death, imprisonment or disbility of the parents.

8. A person who removes an Indian child from his/her home may place the child in a temporary home, to be chosen at the discretion of the person removing the Indian child.

9. A person who removes an Indian child from his/her home shall within seven days bring the child before Chief and Council.

10. Before deciding where the Indian child should be placed, Chief and Council should consider and be guided by Indian customs and the following preferences.

(i) The wishes of the Indian child, whenever, in the opinion of Band Council, the child is old enough to appreciate his/her situation.

(ii) Wherever possible, help should be given to rebuild the family of the Indian child.

(iii) In the absence of placement with the family, a preference for placement shall be given in this order to:

1) a parent.

2) a member of the extended family living on the reserve.

3) a member of the extended family living on another reserve, although not a reserve of the Indian Band.

4) a member of the extended family living off the reserve.

5) an Indian living on a reserve.

6) an Indian living off a reserve.

7) only as a last resort shall the child be placed in the home of a non-Indian living off the reserve.

(iv) In all cases, the best interests of the child should be the deciding consideration.

11. The Chief and Council shall place the child in a suitable home.

12. Any Band member or any parent or member of the Indian child's extended family or Indian guardian may review the decision made by the Band Council to remove the Indian child from his/her home or to the placement of the child by Band Council.

13. The person seeking a review shall notify in writing Band Council at least 14 days before the next band meeting.

14. Upon receiving the written notice to review, Band Council shall put the question before the Indian Band at the next General Band meeting.

15. The Indian Band, by majority vote of the Band members attending at the General Band meeting shall decide on the placement of the Indian child. The decision of the Indian Band shall be governed by the considerations stated in S. 10 of this by-law.

16. The Chief and Council shall ensure that the child's family be advised of important changes and events in the life of the child while the child is in the care of the Band. Wherever possible the responsibility for such communications shall be delegated to the Indian guardian.

17. The Chief and Council shall ensure that an assistance programme be established from time to time, which may be necessary to facilitate the stable placement of an Indian child.

18. The Indian child, the parent, member of extended family or Indian guardian may, at any time seek a decision from Band Council concerning the return of the Indian child to his/her family, or the removal of the Indian child to the home of another Indian guardian.

19. Upon receiving written notice of an application to return or remove the Indian child, the Band Council shall consider the placement, guided by the consideration under S. 10 of this by-law to return the Indian child to his/her family or maintain the Indian child with the Indian guardian or place the Indian child in another home.

20. Any Band member, parent, member of the child's extended family or Indian guardian may review Band Council's decision under S. 19 of the by-law.

21. The person reviewing shall notify Band Council in writing at least 14 days before the next General Band Meeting.

22. Upon receiving written notice to review, Band Council shall put the question before the Indian Band at the next General Band meeting.

23. The Indian Band by majority vote of the Band Members attending the General Band Meeting, shall decide on the placement of the Indian child. The decision of the Band shall be made and governed by the consideration under S. 10 of this by-law.

This by-law was passed by a unanimous vote of Band Members at a General Band meeting held April 22, 1980 held at the Timbercreek Council Hall; and a unanimous vote of Band Council, taken at that General Band meeting. . . .

BIBLIOGRAPHY

Alberta, Office of the Ombudsman. "An Investigation by the Alberta Ombudsman into the Foster Care Program." Edmonton, March 1981.

Andres, Renate. "The Apprehension of Native Children." *Ontario Indian*, vol. 4, no. 5 (April 1981).

Angus, Albert. "The Thunderchild." *Queen's Journal Magazine*, vol. 3 no. 1 (November 1981).

Association on American Indian Affairs. *Indian Family Defense: A Bulletin of the Association on American Indian Affairs*, no. 11. New York, February 1979.

Bagley, Chris. "Total Child Welfare for The Eighties." Paper prepared for The Canadian Child in the Eighties Conference, 18-20 March 1981, at Mount Saint Vincent University, Halifax.

Barsh, Russel Lawrence. "The BIA Reorganization Follies of 1978: A Lesson in Bureaucratic Self Defence." *American Indian Law Review*, vol. 7, no. 1 (1979).

"The Indian Child Welfare Act of 1978: A Critical Analysis." *Hastings Law Journal,* vol. 31 (July 1980), pp. 1287-1336.

Battel, Mildred. *Children Shall Be First: Child Welfare Saskatchewan, 1944-1964.* Regina: Published with the assistance of the Saskatchewan Department of Culture and Youth, 1979.

Berger, Mr. Justice Thomas R. *Northern Frontier, Northern Homeland —The Report of the MacKenzie Valley Pipeline Inquiry*, vol. 1. Ottawa: Canada Department of Supply and Services, 1977.

Blanchard, Evelyn Lance, and Barsh, Russel Lawrence. "What is Best for Tribal Children?" *Social Work*, vol. 25, no. 5 (September 1980).

Blaney, Fay. *Final Report on the Terms of Reference to the Child Welfare Committee.* Vancouver: Union of British Columbia Indian Chiefs, June 1980.

Bobiwash, Libby, and Malloch, Lesley. *A Family Needs Survey.* Toronto: Native Canadian Centre of Toronto, 1980.

Breton, Raymond, and Akian, Gail Grant. *Urban Institutions and People of Indian Ancestry.* Montreal: Institute for Research on Public Policy, 1978.

Briggs, Jean. *Aspects of Inuit Value Socialization,* Mercury Series, paper no. 56. Ottawa: National Museums of Canada, 1979.

British Columbia, Royal Commission on Family and Children's Law. *Fifth Report of the Royal Commission on Family and Children's Law: Part VII — Adoption.* Vancouver, March 1975.

British Columbia. *Tenth Report of the Royal Commission on Family and Children's Law: Native Families and the Law.* Vancouver, May 1975.

British Columbia Native Women's Society, "Proposal for Recommended Legislative Enactment with Respect to Rights for Native Indian Children and Protection of Native Indian Children by Independent Indian Bands." Proposal presented at the society's annual conference, Kamloops, 1979.

Brody, Hugh. *The People's Land.* Toronto: Penguin Books, 1975.

Canada, Department of Indian Affairs and Northern Development. *Statement of the Government of Canada on Indian Policy 1969.* Ottawa, 1969.

Canada, Department of Indian and Northern Affairs. *The Historical Development of the Indian Act.* Ottawa, 1978.

Indian Conditions: A Survey. Ottawa, 1980.

Canadian Commission for the International Year of the Child, 1979. *For Canada's Children. Ottawa, 1980.*

Canadian Council on Children and Youth. *Admittance Restricted: The Child as Citizen in Canada.* Ottawa, 1978.

Legislation Related to the Needs of Children: A Legislative Appendix to Admittance Restricted. Toronto: Carswell Co., 1979.

Canadian Welfare Council and Canadian Association of Social Workers."Joint Submission to the Special Joint Committee of the Senate and the House of Commons Appointed to Examine and Consider The Indian Act." Ottawa: Canadian Welfare Council, 1947.

Center for Social Research and Development. *Indian Child Welfare, A State-of-the-Field Study: Summary of Findings and Discussion of Policy Implications.* Denver: University of Denver, August 1976.

Daniels, Harry W., ed. *The Forgotten People.* Ottawa: Native Council of Canada, 1979.

Daniels, Harry W. *We Are the New Nation: The Métis and National Native Policy.* Ottawa: Native Council of Canada, 1979.

Family Service Association of America. *Social Casework*, vol. 61, no. 8 (October 1980).

Fanshel, David. *Far From the Reservation: The Transracial Adoption of American Indian Children.* Methuen, N.J.: Scarescrow Press, 1972.

Fischler, Ronald S. "Protecting American Indian Children." *Social Work*, vol. 25, no. 5 (September 1980).

Freeman, Minnie Aodla. *Life Among the Quallunat.* Edmonton: Hurtig, 1978.

Geumple, Lee. *Inuit Adoption*, paper no. 47, Mercury Series. Ottawa: National Museums of Canada, 1979.

Gilman, Susan. "The Native Child." Ottawa: Canadian Commission for the International Year of the Child, 1979.

Guerrero, Manuel P. "Indian Child Welfare Act of 1978: A Response to the Threat to Indian Culture Caused by Foster and Adoptive Placements of Indian Children." *American Indian Law Review*, vol. 7, no. 1 (1979).

Harrington, Richard. *The Inuit: Life as It Was.* Edmonton: Hurtig, 1981.

Hawthorn, H. B., ed. *A Survey of the Contemporary Indians of Canada: A Report on Economic, Political, Educational Needs and Policies*, vol. 1, 2. Ottawa: Canada Department of Indian Affairs and Northern Development, 1966.

Hepworth, H. Philip. *Foster Care and Adoption in Canada.* Ottawa: Canadian Council on Social Development, 1980.

Hudson, Peter, and McKenzie, Brad. "Child Welfare and Native People: The Extension of Colonialism." *Social Worker*, vol. 49, no. 2 (Summer 1981).

Indian Child Welfare Workshop, Winnipeg, 1980. *Summary of Proceedings.* Winnipeg: Canadian Indian Lawyers Association, 1980.

Indian Homemakers' Association of British Columbia. "The Family Unit Concept." Vancouver 1981.

Jenness, Diamond. *The Indians of Canada*, 3rd ed. Ottawa: Canada Department of Northern Affairs and Natural Resources, 1955.

Johnson, Barbara Brooks. "The Indian Child Welfare Act of 1978: Implications for Practice." *Child Welfare*, vol. 60, no. 7 (July/August 1981).

"American Indian Jurisdiction as a Policy Issue." *Social Work*, vol. 27, no. 1 (January 1982).

Johnston, Patrick. "Indian Control of Child Welfare A Historic Step." *Perception*, vol. 5, no. 1 (October 1981).

"Indigenous Children at Risk." *Policy Options*, vol. 2, no. 5, (November/December 1981).

"Planting the Roots for Indian Social Services." *Perception*, vol. 5, no. 2 (November/December 1981).

and Novosedlik, Stephen G. "Child Welfare and the Native Peoples of Canada." Paper presented to the Canadian Association of Schools of Social Work Annual Conference, 1-4 June 1982, University of Ottawa.

"The Crisis of Native Child Welfare." *Canadian Legal Aid Bulletin*, vol. 5, nos. 2, 3 (April/July 1982).

Josephy, Alvin M., Jr. *The Indian Heritage of America*. London: Jonathan Cape, 1972.

Krotz, Larry. *Urban Indians: The Strangers in Canada's Cities*. Edmonton: Hurtig, 1980.

LaFontaine, Anne. "Where We Came From: A Review of Traditional Indian Family Life." Ottawa: National Indian Brotherhood, 1979.

Lazore, Melissa. *A Perspective on Contemporary Native People*. Ottawa: Canada Department of Indian and Northern Affairs,1980.

Lewis, Claudia. *Indian Families of the Northwest Coast: The Impact of Change*. Chicago: University of Chicago Press, 1970.

Limprecht, Jane. "The Indian Child Welfare Act — Tribal Self-Determination through Participation in Child Custody Proceedings." *Wisconsin Law Review*, 1979.

Long, J. Anthony; Little Bear, Leroy; and Boldt, Menno. "Federal Indian Policy and Indian Self-Government in Canada: An Analysis of a Current Proposal." *Canadian Public Policy*, vol. 8, no. 2 (Spring 1982).

MacDonald, John A. "The Spallumcheen Indian Band By-Law and Its Potential Impact on Native Indian Child Welfare Policy in British Columbia." Vancouver: School of Social Work, University of British Columbia, April 1981.

Manitoba, Child Welfare Directorate. "The Manitoba Indian Adoption Program." Information given to the sixth meeting of the National Commission Inquiry on Indian Health, March 1980.

Manitoba Métis Federation. "Position Paper on Child Care and Family Services." Winnipeg, May 1982.

Manitoba Tripartite Committee. *Report of the Indian Child Welfare Subcommittee — Manitoba.* Winnipeg, March 1980.

Marousek, Linda A. "The Indian Child Welfare Act of 1978: Provisions and Policy." *South Dakota Law Review*, vol. 25 (Winter 1980).

McKenzie, Brad. "Indian Child Welfare Studied." *Perception,* January/February 1981.

McMullen, Mary Charlotte. "Preserving the Indian Family." *Children's Legal Rights Journal,* vol. 2, no. 6 (May/June 1981).

Mercredi, Ovide, and Chartier, Clem. "The Status of Child Welfare Services for the Indigenous Peoples of Canada: The Problem, The Law and The Solution," Presented at Indian Child Welfare Rights Conference, March 1981.

Metcalf, Ann. "A Model for Treatment in A Native American Family Service Center." Oakland Calif.: Urban Indian Child Resource Center, December 1978.

Moore, William M.; Silverberg, Marjorie M.; and Read, Merrill S. *Nutrition, Growth and Development of North American Indian Children.* DHEW publication no. (NIH) 72-26. Washington: U.S. Government Printing Office, 1972.

Morey, Sylvester M., and Gilliam, Olivia L., eds.. *Respect for Life: Report of a Conference at Harper's Ferry, West Virginia, on the Traditional Upbringing of American Indian Children.* Garden City, N.Y.: Waldorf Press, 1972.

Morse, Bradford W. "Indian Child Welfare: A Tragedy in Need of Reform." Paper presented to Conference on Provincial Social Welfare Policy, 5-7 May 1982, Faculty of Social Welfare, University of Calgary.

National Council of Welfare. *In the Best Interests of the Child: A Report by the National Council of Welfare on the Child Welfare System in Canada.* Ottawa, December 1979.

Native Canadian Centre of Toronto."Our Position on Native Child and Family Welfare in Toronto." Toronto, November 1980.

Native Law Association Conference, Vancouver, 1979. "Summary of Proceedings."

Novosedlik, Stephen G. "Child Welfare and the Indigenous Peoples of Canada: A Compelling Case for Legislative Discrimination." M.S.W. thesis, Carleton University, 1982.

Ontario, Ministry of Community and Social Services. *Foster Care: Proposed Standards and Guidelines for Agencies Placing Children*. Toronto, 1981.

Ponting, J. Rick, and Gibbins, Roger. *Out of Irrelevance: A Socio-Political Introduction to Indian Affairs in Canada*. Toronto: Butterworths, 1980.

Rausch, Carl. "Native Child Welfare and Paulo Freire: Shaping a More Humane and Just World for Native Family Life in Southern Alberta." M.S.W. thesis, University of Calgary, 1982.

Read, Peter. "The Stolen Generations: The Removal of Aboriginal Children in New South Wales, 1883 - 1969." Discussion paper presented by Aboriginal Childrens' Research Project, 1981, Sydney, Australia.

Sanders, Douglas. *Family Law and Native Peoples: Background Paper*. Ottawa: Law Reform Commission of Canada, 1975.

Siggner, Andrew J. *An Overview of Demographic Social and Economic Conditions among Canada's Registered Indian Population*. Ottawa: Indian and Inuit Affairs Program, September 1979.

Sinclair, Murray. "The Child Welfare Act of Manitoba and the Role of the Extended Family." Discussion paper prepared for Indian Child Welfare Rights Workshop, March 1981, Regina.

Sissons, Jack. *Judge of the Far North*. Toronto: McClelland and Stewart, 1968.

Soiseth, Len. "A Community that Cares for Children." *Canadian Welfare*, vol. 46, no. 3 (May/June 1970).

Steward, Kate Jo. "The Indian Child Welfare Act" Los Angeles: Indian Centers Inc., 1981.

Stuart Neil. "Study of Child Welfare Services Provided to Indian People in The Sudbury and Manitoulin District." M.S.W. thesis, Carleton University, 1978.

Technical Assistance and Planning Associates, Ltd. *A Starving Man Doesn't Argue: A Review of Community Social Services to Indians in Ontario*. Toronto, July 1979.

Technical Assistance and Planning Associates, Ltd. *Toward Indian Community Control of Indian Social Services*. Toronto, 1980.

Unger, Steven, ed. *The Destruction of American Indian Families*. New York: Association on American Indian Affairs, 1977.

United States. Indian Child Welfare Act of 1978. Public Law 95-608, 92 Stat. 3069, 95th Congress.

Wamser, Garry. "Child Welfare under the Indian Child Welfare Act of 1978: A New Mexico Focus." *New Mexico Law Review*, vol. 10 Summer 1980.

Weaver, Sally M. *Making Canadian Indian Policy: The Hidden Agenda 1968-70*. Toronto: University of Toronto Press, 1981.

Wuerscher, Rose. *Problems with the Legislative Base for Native Indian Child Welfare Services*. Ottawa: Canada Department of Indian and Northern Affairs, 1979.